Cookie Jar Magic

Magical Cookie Dough,

Gifts In A Jar &

Cookie Cutter Fun

Lia Roessner Wilson

Published by

cookbook resources LLC

Cookie Jar Magic

1st Printing   August 2003

ISBN 1-931294-52-6

Library of Congress Number: 2003110342

Illustrated by Nancy Murphy Griffith
Art Direction by Liz Reinken
Graphic Design by Fit to Print

Edited, Designed, Published and Manufactured in the
United States of America by
Cookbook Resources, LLC
541 Doubletree Drive
Highland Village, Texas 75077
Toll free 866-229-2665
www.cookbookresources.com

cookbook
resources LLC

★ Cookie Jar Magic ★

There really is magic in every cookie jar no matter its size, color or shape. The magic jumps out of the jar and into the hands of a little kid (regardless of age), then straight into a mouth that remembers all the smells and flavors rolled into a few wonderful bites. In this jar of magic, there are three kinds of magic: magic dough, magic ingredients and magic shapes. Read along to see if you will make your own kind of magic for a jar on the counter by the window next to the napkins.

Magical Cookie Dough turns into 70 different cookies at the snap of your fingers!

Yes, there really is one basic cookie dough that can become at least 70 different cookies just with the addition of a few everyday ingredients. This is great because all you have to do for fresh, hot homemade cookies is to have the basic cookie dough in the freezer. Thaw it out, add your magic and taste the goodness in *White Chocolate Cherry Rounds, Peanut Butter and Jelly Thumbprint Cookies, Peppermint Candy Cane Cookies, Pecan Whirls, Apple Pie Bites* and *Chocolate Fudge Thumbprints*.

Magical Ingredients put in a jar in nice, neat layers make great gifts and fundraisers at bake sales and school fairs!

Everybody loves recipes in a jar. Just empty the contents, stir in a few ingredients and bake delicious cookies with minimal time and effort. *Malted Milk Crunchies, Butterscotch Snaps, Chocolate Snickerdoodles, Orange Sugar Cookies* and *Walnut Cinnamon Balls* are just the best kind of magic you may eat.

Magical Shapes, Colors and Sizes make our cookie cutter recipes an afternoon of fun and memories!

Make sure you have trees, bunnies, hearts, bells, ponies, gingerbread men, Santas and tons of other special shapes for those special little kids with stars in their eyes and smiles on their faces. You will fill their hearts and their tummies with the memories of colored sprinkles, special icings and heart-shaped candies sitting on top of the special cookies they get to make. Work your own kind of magic for the holidays and special occasions with magical shapes, colors and flavors in *Ornament Cookies, Chocolate Trees, Gingerbread Army, Crusty Cut-Outs* and *Sweetheart Cookies*.

There's magic in that cookie jar...your magic ...your homemade goodness ★

Contents

Cookie Dough Secrets
★ Part I ★

Cookie Cutter Recipes
★ Part II ★

Contents

Gifts For The Cookie Jar
★ Part III ★

PART I

Cookie Dough Secrets

1 Basic Cookie Dough

10 Cookie Recipes

♥

Lia Roessner Wilson

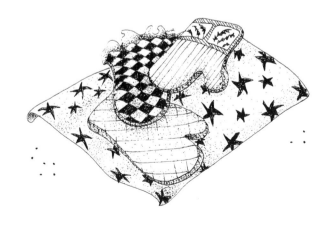

70 Easy to Make, Distinctive Cookies from One Dough
♥ ♥ ♥

By adding as few as 2 or 3 ingredients to our simple, Basic Cookie Dough, you can create 70 delicious cookies in many shapes and sizes.

Look for this helpful heart because it shows you the really fast and easy recipes.

All these cookie recipes are easy to make. Although it's not necessary, you can make the dough ahead of time and keep it refrigerated until you're ready to bake. Just take it out, warm it up and you're halfway to having fresh, hot cookies. You can even freeze the dough for up to several weeks. Just thaw, bring it to room temperature and you're good to go!

The recipes on the pages that follow give you flexibility in the types of cookies you can make. Don't have a lot of time? Choose one of the drop cookie recipes and whip up a batch in minutes.

Want something a little more out of the ordinary? Pick a pinwheel recipe or a shaped cookie and create a treat that's a little unique.

Looking for something more tasty than store-bought sandwich cookies? Try a jam or creme-filled sandwich cookie recipe. These are just the thing to take to a holiday gathering, serve to the kids as an afternoon snack or give to neighbors as a thoughtful gift.

You'll be amazed at the variety that can be made from one simple dough.

Contents - PART I

Contents – PART I

Author Lia Roessner Wilson has a general love of cooking, but is passionate about baking. A member of the IACP (International Association of Culinary Professionals) and a seasoned cook, she creates extraordinary desserts delightful enough for entertaining, yet simple enough for every day. Her first cookbook, Quick Fixes with Mixes, has been showcased several times on QVC.

Lia's most enjoyable role is that of mother to her two sons. She is a mom who believes in making memories for them through the wonderful aromas and treats from her kitchen – the kind of memories that will be treasured for a lifetime.

Basic Cookie Dough

$1/2$ cup (1 stick) butter or margarine, softened
1 cup sugar
1 egg
$1/2$ teaspoon vanilla
$1/2$ teaspoon salt
1 teaspoon baking powder
2 cups flour

In large bowl, cream butter and sugar. Add egg and vanilla and beat until light and fluffy.

In medium bowl, sift salt, baking powder and flour together. Gradually add to butter mixture, beating well after each addition.

Cover and refrigerate dough until ready to use. Warm to room temperature before using unless recipe specifies otherwise.

Chocolate-Topped Brownie Bites

Looking and tasting like little bits of brownie, these cookies are fast to make and will disappear even faster.

1 recipe Basic Cookie Dough
4 tablespoons cocoa powder
$1/2$ cup milk
$1/2$ cup chopped nuts
1 cup coconut

Preheat oven to 350°. In medium bowl, combine Basic Cookie Dough with cocoa powder and milk. Beat on low speed to blend.

Stir in nuts and coconut.

Drop by rounded teaspoonfuls onto lightly greased cookie sheet. Bake for 10 minutes. Remove from oven and let cookies cool on cookie sheet for 1 minute, then transfer to cooling rack. When cool, spoon about 1 teaspoon chocolate glaze over the top of each cookie. Let chocolate set before serving or storing. (Makes 4 to 4 $1/2$ dozen.)

Chocolate Glaze

1 cup semi-sweet chocolate chips
6 tablespoons margarine or
    shortening

Combine chocolate and shortening in small saucepan and melt over very low heat, stirring constantly until mixture is smooth. Remove from heat and use immediately.

Brandied Fruitcake Cookies

A hearty, holiday cookie that's big on fruitcake flavor. These will appeal to those who like fruitcake flavor but aren't crazy about spices. They have a moist texture and their light color lets the colorful fruits and nuts show through.

♥ ♥ ♥

1/2 cup brandy
1 cup fruitcake mix (candied fruit)
1 recipe Basic Cookie Dough
1 tablespoon buttermilk
1 teaspoon orange extract
1 cup chopped pecans
1 cup raisins

In small saucepan, heat brandy almost to boiling. Pour over fruitcake mix and let sit for 20 minutes. Drain and reserve brandy. Set fruit aside.

Preheat oven to 375°. In medium bowl, combine Basic Cookie Dough with reserved brandy, buttermilk and orange extract. Beat until dough is well blended.

Stir in fruit, pecans and raisins.

Drop by heaping teaspoonfuls onto lightly greased cookie sheet. Bake for 10 to 12 minutes or until lightly browned around edges.

Remove from oven and let cookies cool on cookie sheet for 1 minute, then transfer to cooling rack. (Makes 4 to 5 dozen.)

Basic Cookie Dough Recipe on Page 7

Spicy Pineapple Cookies

1 recipe Basic Cookie Dough
1 teaspoon cinnamon
$1/2$ teaspoon ground nutmeg
$1/4$ teaspoon ground cloves
$2/3$ cup crushed pineapple, very well drained

Preheat oven to 375°. In medium bowl, combine Basic Cookie
Dough with cinnamon, nutmeg, cloves and pineapple. Beat until
dough is thoroughly blended.

Drop by heaping teaspoonfuls onto ungreased cookie sheet. Bake
for 13 to 15 minutes or until edges are lightly browned. Remove
from oven and let cookies cool on cookie sheet for 1 minute, then
transfer to cooling rack. (Makes 3 $1/2$ to 4 dozen.)

Maple Iced Walnut Drops

Real maple syrup is the key to making these tasty cookies. It gives the icing a strong maple flavor that complements the flavor of the walnuts in the cookies. These take very little time to make, especially if you whip up the icing while the first batch is baking.

1 recipe Basic Cookie Dough
2 cups coarsely chopped walnuts

Preheat oven to 350°. In medium bowl, mix walnuts with Basic Cookie Dough.

Drop by heaping teaspoonfuls onto ungreased cookie sheet. Bake for 10 to 12 minutes or until lightly browned around edges.

Remove from oven and let cookies cool on cookie sheet for 1 minute, then transfer to cooling rack. When cool, frost with maple icing.

Maple Icing

3 tablespoons butter or
    margarine, softened
1 1/2 cups powdered sugar
1/4 cup maple syrup

Combine butter, powdered sugar and maple syrup in medium bowl. Beat until well blended and mixture is smooth.

Basic Cookie Dough Recipe on Page 7

11

Mocha Chip Drops

These light cookies have a delicate mocha flavor and are studded with chocolate chips.

 1 teaspoon instant coffee
 2 tablespoons half-and-half or milk
 1 recipe Basic Cookie Dough
 $^1/_2$ cup shortening
 $^1/_2$ teaspoon almond extract
 1 cup mini-chocolate chips

Preheat oven to 375°. In small bowl, stir coffee into half-and-half to dissolve. Set aside.

In medium bowl, combine Basic Cookie Dough with shortening, almond extract and coffee mixture. Beat until dough is well blended.

Stir in chocolate chips.

Drop by heaping teaspoonfuls onto ungreased cookie sheet. Bake for 10 minutes. Remove from oven and let cookies cool on cookie sheet for 1 minute, then transfer to cooling rack. (Makes 4 to 4 $^1/_2$ dozen.)

Spicy Iced Pumpkin Drops

One of my favorite recipes, this slightly cake-like cookie has a wonderful flavor and moist texture. One of its best features is that it keeps very well if tightly covered. The flavor just gets better as the cookies sit for a day or so.

♥ ♥ ♥

1 recipe Basic Cookie Dough
$^1/_2$ cup shortening
1 cup canned pumpkin
$^1/_2$ teaspoon baking soda

1 teaspoon cinnamon
$^1/_2$ teaspoon ground nutmeg
1 cup coarsely chopped walnuts
1 cup raisins

Preheat oven to 350°. In large bowl, combine Basic Cookie Dough with shortening, pumpkin, baking soda, cinnamon and nutmeg. Beat until dough is well blended.

Stir in walnuts and raisins.

Drop by heaping teaspoonfuls onto ungreased cookie sheet. Bake for 15 minutes. Remove from oven and let cookies cool on cookie sheet for 1 minute, then transfer to cooling rack. (Makes 4 to 5 dozen.)

When cool, ice with Orange Frosting.

Orange Frosting

2 cups powdered sugar
$^1/_2$ cup butter or margarine, softened
4 tablespoons orange juice

In medium bowl, cream sugar and butter. Beat in orange juice and mix until mixture is smooth. (You may want to add a bit more or less orange juice to get the consistency you want.)

Basic Cookie Dough Recipe on Page 7

White Chocolate Cherry Rounds

1 recipe Basic Cookie Dough
¼ cup shortening
¼ cup packed brown sugar
1 tablespoon milk
1 cup white chocolate chips
1 cup chopped maraschino cherries, drained, patted dry

Preheat oven to 375°. In large bowl, combine Basic Cookie Dough with shortening, brown sugar and milk. Beat until well-blended.

Stir in white chocolate chips and cherries.

Drop by heaping teaspoonfuls onto ungreased cookie sheet. Bake for 10 to 12 minutes, just until edges begin to brown.

Remove from oven and let cookies cool on cookie sheet for 1 minute. Transfer to cooling rack. (Makes 3 to 4 dozen.)

Pfeffernuesse

1 recipe Basic Cookie Dough
$1/4$ cup buttermilk
$1/4$ cup molasses
$1/2$ teaspoon ginger
$1/2$ teaspoon cinnamon
$1/4$ teaspoon ground cloves
$1/4$ teaspoon black pepper

Preheat oven to 350°. In medium bowl, combine Basic Cookie Dough with buttermilk, molasses, ginger, cinnamon, cloves and pepper. Beat until dough is thoroughly blended.

Drop by rounded teaspoonfuls onto lightly greased cookie sheet. Bake for 10 minutes or until edges are lightly browned.

Remove from oven and let cookies cool on cookie sheet for 1 minute, then transfer to cooling rack. (Makes 4 dozen.)

Basic Cookie Dough Recipe on Page 7

Applesauce Drops

A moist, cake-like cookie loaded with texture and the sweet taste of apples. They have a light, delicate flavor.

1 recipe Basic Cookie Dough
$1/2$ cup packed brown sugar
1 cup applesauce
2 cups quick-cooking oats
1 cup raisins

Preheat oven to 375°. In medium bowl, combine Basic Cookie Dough with brown sugar, applesauce and oats. Beat until well blended. Stir in raisins.

Drop by rounded teaspoonfuls onto lightly greased cookie sheet.

Bake for 10 to 12 minutes or until lightly browned around edges. Remove from oven and let cookies cool on cookie sheet for 1 minute, then transfer to cooling rack. (Makes $3^1/2$ to 4 dozen.)

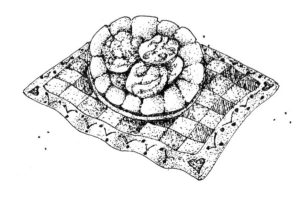

Brandy-Dipped Apricot Delights

$^1/_2$ cup brandy
1 cup chopped dried apricots
1 recipe Basic Cookie Dough
1 tablespoon buttermilk

In small saucepan, heat brandy almost to boiling. Pour over apricots and set aside for 20 minutes to soften. Drain and reserve brandy. Set apricots aside.

Preheat oven to 375°. In medium bowl, combine Basic Cookie Dough with buttermilk and reserved brandy. Beat until dough is well-blended. Stir in apricots.

Drop by heaping teaspoonfuls onto lightly greased cookie sheet. Bake for 10 to 12 minutes, just until edges begin to brown.

Remove from oven and let cookies cool on cookie sheet for 1 minute, then transfer to cooling rack. When cool, frost with Brandy Icing. To frost, either dip cookies in the icing, letting excess drip off and then place on wax paper to set. Or, you can put a sheet of wax paper under cooling rack and spoon icing over cookies, letting wax paper catch drips.

Brandy Icing

3 cups powdered sugar
3 tablespoons milk
4-5 tablespoons brandy

In medium bowl, combine powdered sugar with milk and brandy. Beat until icing mixture is smooth. Add additional powdered sugar if icing is too thin or additional brandy if it's too thick.

Basic Cookie Dough Recipe on Page 7

Hearty Carrot Cookies

These scrumptious, cake-like little treats cause very little guilt when I eat more than I should. Loaded with healthy ingredients like carrots, oats and raisins, how can they be anything but good for you?

1 recipe Basic Cookie Dough
$1/2$ cup packed brown sugar
1 cup shredded, peeled carrots
1 teaspoon cinnamon
$1/2$ teaspoon ground nutmeg
2 cups quick-cooking oats
1 cup raisins
1 cup coarsely chopped walnuts or pecans

Preheat oven to 375°. In large bowl, combine Basic Cookie Dough with brown sugar, carrots, cinnamon and nutmeg. Beat until well blended. Beat in oats. Stir in raisins and nuts.

Drop by heaping teaspoonfuls onto lightly greased cookie sheet and bake for 10 minutes or until lightly browned around edges.

Remove from oven and let cookies cool on cookie sheet for 1 minute, then transfer to cooling rack. (Makes 4 $1/2$ to 5 dozen.)

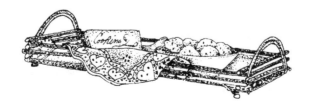

Banana Cookies with Banana Frosting

These cookies are light and crispy with a bold banana flavor! For even better flavor, toast the nuts before adding to the dough by baking on a cookie sheet for 5 minutes at 350°. These also taste great either with or without the frosting.

1 recipe Basic Cookie Dough
$^1/_2$ cup shortening
$^1/_2$ cup packed brown sugar

$^3/_4$ cup mashed ripe bananas
$^2/_3$ cup quick-cooking oats
1 cup chopped nuts (optional)

Preheat oven to 350°. In large bowl, combine Basic Cookie Dough with shortening, brown sugar and bananas and mix thoroughly. Blend in oats. Stir in nuts (if you want).

Drop by heaping teaspoonfuls onto ungreased cookie sheet and bake for 15 minutes, or until edges are lightly browned.

Remove from oven and let cookies cool on cookie sheet for 1 minute, then transfer to cooling rack. (Makes 4 $^1/_2$ to 5 dozen.)

When cool, ice with Banana Frosting.

Banana Frosting

2 tablespoons butter or margarine, softened
$^1/_4$ cup mashed ripe bananas
1 teaspoon lemon juice
2 cups powdered sugar

In medium bowl, cream butter, bananas and lemon juice until smooth. Add powdered sugar one cup at a time blending well after each addition. Beat until smooth.

Basic Cookie Dough Recipe on Page 7

Date-Studded Orange Cookies

Another winning flavor combination, dates, orange and cinnamon go together like they were made for each other. They're all in this easy to make, but fabulous, cookie. If dates aren't handy, or aren't your preference, substitute raisins instead. You'll get the same great flavor.

♥ ♥ ♥

1 recipe Basic Cookie Dough
$^1/_2$ cup shortening
$^1/_2$ cup packed brown sugar
$^1/_2$ teaspoon baking soda
1 teaspoon cinnamon
2 tablespoons orange zest
1 egg white
1 cup chopped dates
$^1/_2$ cup coconut

Preheat oven to 375°. In large bowl, combine shortening, brown sugar, baking soda, cinnamon, orange zest and egg white with Basic Cookie Dough. Beat until well blended.

Stir in dates and coconut.

Drop by heaping teaspoonfuls onto ungreased cookie sheet. Bake for 10 to 12 minutes or until nicely browned.

Remove from oven and let cookies cool on cookie sheet for 1 minute before transferring to cooling rack. (Makes 4 to 4 $^1/_2$ dozen.)

Crispy Pecan Thins

These thin little cookies are crisp and crunchy. If you like the taste of cinnamon, add half a teaspoonful to the dough along with the other ingredients.

1 recipe Basic Cookie Dough
$^1/_2$ cup shortening
$^3/_4$ cup packed brown sugar
$^1/_2$ teaspoon baking soda
1 egg white
1 $^1/_2$ cups coarsely chopped pecans

Preheat oven to 375°. In large bowl, combine shortening, brown sugar, baking soda and egg white with Basic Cookie Dough. Beat until well blended.

Stir in pecans.

Drop by heaping teaspoonfuls onto ungreased cookie sheet. Bake for 12 to 14 minutes or until nicely browned all over.

Remove from oven and let cookies cool on cookie sheet for 1 minute before transferring to cooling rack. (Makes 4 to 4 $^1/_2$ dozen.)

Basic Cookie Dough Recipe on Page 7

Oatmeal Raisin Cookies

1 recipe Basic Cookie Dough
$^1/_2$ cup shortening
$^1/_2$ cup packed brown sugar
$^1/_2$ teaspoon baking soda
1 egg white
$^3/_4$ cup quick-cooking oats
$^3/_4$ cup raisins

Preheat oven to 375°. In large bowl, combine shortening, brown sugar, baking soda and egg white with Basic Cookie Dough. Beat until well blended.

Stir in oats and raisins.

Drop by heaping teaspoonfuls onto ungreased cookie sheet. Bake for 10 to 12 minutes or until nicely browned.

Remove from oven and let cookies cool on cookie sheet for 1 minute before transferring to cooling rack. (Makes 4 to 4 $^1/_2$ dozen.)

Hearty Trail Mix Cookies

There are several varieties of trail mix. I like to find one with colorful chocolate candies, nuts and raisins, but you can use any that appeal to you. You can even make your own if you want. Simply mix together a variety of nuts, chocolate candy or chocolate chips, raisins or other dried fruit in equal proportions.

1 recipe Basic Cookie Dough
$1/2$ cup shortening
$1/2$ cup packed brown sugar
$1/2$ teaspoon baking soda
1 egg white
1 $1/2$ cups trail mix
$3/4$ cup coconut

Preheat oven to 375°. In large bowl, combine shortening, brown sugar, baking soda and egg white with Basic Cookie Dough. Beat until well blended.

Stir in trail mix and coconut.

Drop by heaping teaspoonfuls onto ungreased cookie sheet. Bake for 10 to 12 minutes or until nicely browned.

Remove from oven and let cookies cool on cookie sheet for 1 minute before transferring to cooling rack. (Makes 4 to 4 $1/2$ dozen.)

Basic Cookie Dough Recipe on Page 7

Apple Cranberry Cookies

Apples and cranberries are a wonderful combination and seem especially suited to the Thanksgiving and Christmas holidays. These chunky cookies pack a lot of punch in a small treat. With their spicy flavor and attractive red and white colors, these cookies are great during the holiday season. Try adding a cup of white chocolate chips for a little variety.

1 recipe Basic Cookie Dough
$1/2$ cup shortening
$1/2$ cup packed brown sugar
$1/2$ teaspoon baking soda
1 egg white
$1/4$ teaspoon ground nutmeg
$1/2$ teaspoon cinnamon
$1/4$ teaspoon lemon extract
$3/4$ cup coarsely chopped walnuts
$3/4$ cup dried, sweetened cranberries
$3/4$ cup chopped dried apples

Preheat oven to 375°. In large bowl, combine shortening, brown sugar, baking soda, egg white, nutmeg, cinnamon and lemon extract with Basic Cookie Dough and beat until well blended.

Stir in walnuts, cranberries and dried apples.

Drop by heaping teaspoonfuls onto lightly greased cookie sheet. Bake for 10 to 12 minutes or until nicely browned.

Remove from oven and let cookies cool on cookie sheet for 1 minute before transferring to cooling rack. (Makes 4 to 4 $1/2$ dozen.)

Ranger Cookies

1 recipe Basic Cookie Dough
$^1/_2$ cup shortening
1 cup packed brown sugar
1 egg
1 teaspoon baking soda
3 cups crisped rice cereal

Preheat oven to 350°. In large bowl, combine Basic Cookie Dough with shortening, brown sugar, egg and baking soda. Beat until well mixed.

Stir in crisped rice.

Drop by heaping teaspoonfuls onto ungreased cookie sheet.

Bake for 10 to 12 minutes or until edges are lightly browned. Remove from oven and let cookies cool on cookie sheet for 1 minute before transferring to cooling rack. (Makes 4 to 4 $^1/_2$ dozen.)

Basic Cookie Dough Recipe on Page 7

Lemon Zucchini Cookies

Anyone who likes zucchini bread will like the taste of these. Nutty and cake like, these cookies are light in flavor and texture. The slight citrus flavor goes really well with the zucchini.

1 recipe Basic Cookie Dough
$^1/_2$ cup shortening
$^1/_2$ teaspoon lemon extract
1 cup grated, unpeeled zucchini
1 cup coconut
$^3/_4$ cup chopped walnuts

Preheat oven to 375°. In large bowl, combine shortening with Basic Cookie Dough and blend well. Beat in lemon extract, zucchini and coconut. Stir in walnuts.

Drop by heaping teaspoonfuls onto ungreased cookie sheet.

Bake for 15 to 17 minutes or until edges are lightly browned. Remove from oven and let cookies cool on cookie sheet for 1 minute, then transfer to cooling rack. (Makes 6 to 7 dozen.)

Orange Mocha Drops

One of my favorite flavor combinations, chocolate and orange, is combined in this soft, dense cookie. The chocolate cookie has a hint of coffee flavor and the orange icing is tangy and sweet. This is a great cookie for Halloween, with the dark chocolate of the cookie topped by the orange-colored icing.

1 recipe Basic Cookie Dough
$2/3$ cup sour cream
2 teaspoons instant coffee powder
$1/2$ cup hot water
3 (1 ounce) squares unsweetened chocolate, melted

Preheat oven to 375°. In large bowl, beat Basic Cookie Dough with sour cream. Dissolve coffee in hot water and add to dough mixture, blending well. Beat in melted chocolate.

Drop by rounded teaspoonfuls onto ungreased cookie sheet. Bake for 7 minutes. Immediately after removing from oven, transfer cookies to cooling rack. When cool, frost with Orange Icing. (Makes 4 to 4 $1/2$ dozen.)

Orange Icing

2 tablespoons butter or margarine, melted
2 cups powdered sugar
2 tablespoons milk
1 tablespoon orange zest (grated orange rind)

Combine butter, powdered sugar and milk in small bowl. Beat until mixture is smooth. Stir in orange zest.

Basic Cookie Dough Recipe on Page 7

Orange Glazed Fruitcake Rounds

These spicy cookies are crispy on the edges, but soft on the inside and just bursting with fruitcake flavor. The orange glaze really tops them off and looks really pretty against the dark cookie.

♥ ♥ ♥

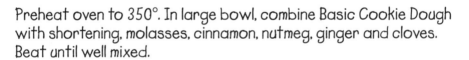

1 recipe Basic Cookie Dough
$1/2$ cup shortening
$1/2$ cup molasses
$1/2$ teaspoon cinnamon
$1/4$ teaspoon ground nutmeg
$1/4$ teaspoon ginger
$1/4$ teaspoon cloves
$1/2$ cup quick-cooking oats
1 cup fruitcake mix (soaked in hot water, well drained & dried)*
1 cup coarsely chopped walnuts (optional)

Preheat oven to 350°. In large bowl, combine Basic Cookie Dough with shortening, molasses, cinnamon, nutmeg, ginger and cloves. Beat until well mixed.

Blend in oats and fruitcake mix (and walnuts, if you want).

Drop by rounded teaspoonful onto ungreased cookie sheet. Bake for 13 to 15 minutes. Remove from oven and let cookies cool on cookie sheet for 1 minute, then transfer to cooling rack.

When cool, drizzle Orange Glaze over cookies in a zigzag motion. To do this, I like to use a small sandwich bag with the corner snipped off. I fill the bag, twist the top above the icing, and then snip a tiny piece off the corner. By gently squeezing the bag, twisting it as necessary to keep pressure on the glaze inside, I can get a neat, steady stream of glaze over the cookies.

Orange Glaze

1 ¹/₂ cups powdered sugar
2 tablespoons orange juice
2 teaspoons orange zest (grated orange rind)

Combine powdered sugar and orange juice in small bowl and beat until mixture is smooth. Stir in orange zest.

*To re-hydrate the fruitcake mix so it's softer in the cookies, I pour boiling water over the mix and let it sit for 20 minutes. Then I drain the water off and dry the mix as much as possible with paper towels.

Basic Cookie Dough Recipe on Page 7

White Chocolate Macadamia Nut Cookies

1 recipe Basic Cookie Dough
$^1/_2$ cup shortening
$^1/_2$ cup packed brown sugar
$^1/_2$ teaspoon baking soda
1 egg white
2 cups white chocolate chips
1 cup coarsely chopped macadamia nuts, toasted

Preheat oven to 375°. In large bowl, combine shortening, brown sugar, baking soda and egg white with Basic Cookie Dough. Beat until well blended.

Stir in white chocolate chips and macadamia nuts.

Drop by heaping teaspoonfuls onto ungreased cookie sheet. Bake for 10 to 12 minutes or until nicely browned.

Remove from oven and let cookies cool on cookie sheet for 1 minute before transferring to cooling rack. (Makes 4 to 4 $^1/_2$ dozen.)

Traditional Chocolate Chip Cookies

1 recipe Basic Cookie Dough
$^1/_2$ cup shortening
$^1/_2$ cup packed brown sugar
$^1/_2$ teaspoon baking soda
1 egg white
2 cups semi-sweet chocolate chips
1 cup chopped pecans or walnuts

Preheat oven to 375°. In large bowl, combine shortening, brown sugar, baking soda, and egg white with Basic Cookie Dough. Beat until well blended.

Stir in chocolate chips and nuts.

Drop heaping teaspoonfuls onto ungreased cookie sheet. Bake for 10 to 12 minutes or until nicely browned.

Remove from oven and let cookies cool on cookie sheet for 1 minute before transferring to cooling rack. (Makes 4 to 4 $^1/_2$ dozen.)

Basic Cookie Dough Recipe on Page 7

Peanut Butter and Jelly Thumbprints

This cookie combines the age-old comfort food favorite peanut butter and jelly, into a delicious cookie that can be made in a snap. Fast and easy!

1 recipe Basic Cookie Dough
1 cup creamy peanut butter
1/2 cup packed brown sugar
3 tablespoons sugar
1/4 cup grape jam or jelly

Preheat oven to 375°. In large bowl, combine Basic Cookie Dough with peanut butter and brown sugar. Beat until well mixed. (The dough will be very stiff.)

Form dough into balls 1 1/2-inch wide. Roll dough balls in sugar and place 2 inches apart on ungreased cookie sheet. Using the back of a blunt handled spoon or your thumb, make an indentation in the top of each ball.

Fill with about 1/2 teaspoon or less of jelly or jam.

Bake for 8 to 10 minutes, just until edges begin to brown, and remove from oven. Let cookies cool for 1 minute on cookie sheet and then transfer to cooling rack. (Makes 3 1/2 to 4 dozen.)

Renna's Cappuccino Drops

What a fun, delicious variation on the peanut butter and chocolate kiss theme! My cousin Renna suggested the combination of coffee, chocolate and white chocolate, and what a hit. The round chocolate cookies look fantastic with the white chocolate kiss sitting on top and they taste great too--just like a smooth cappuccino!

1 recipe Basic Cookie Dough
2 tablespoons shortening
2 tablespoons unsweetened chocolate, melted
2 tablespoons instant coffee powder
2 tablespoons sugar
36-42 white chocolate kisses candies

Preheat oven to 375°. In large bowl, combine shortening, chocolate and coffee powder with Basic Cookie Dough. Mix until well blended and dough is evenly colored.

Place sugar in a shallow dish or bowl.

Form dough into balls 1 ¹/₂ inches in diameter. Roll in sugar to coat, then place 2 inches apart on ungreased cookie sheet. Using your thumb, make a slight indentation in center of each dough ball.

Bake for 5 minutes. Remove from oven and immediately place a candy kiss in the indentation of each cookie, gently pressing down.

Place back in the oven and bake for another 2 minutes. Remove from oven and let cookies cool on cookie sheet for 1 minute, then transfer to cooling rack. (Makes 3 to 3 ¹/₂ dozen.)

Basic Cookie Dough Recipe on Page 7

Chocolate Covered Cherry Delights

What a rich, delicious cookie that's more like candy. The chocolate forms a nice candy-like coating over the dense chocolate cookie. They stay really moist if kept tightly covered.

1 recipe Basic Cookie Dough
2 (1 ounce) squares unsweetened chocolate, melted
36 to 42 maraschino cherries, well drained
    (about one 16-ounce jar)
1 cup semi-sweet chocolate chips
1/2 cup sweetened condensed milk
1 tablespoon maraschino cherry juice

Preheat oven to 350°. In medium bowl, combine melted chocolate with Basic Cookie Dough and beat until well-blended.

Roll pieces of dough into balls about 1 1/2 inches in diameter and place 2 inches apart on ungreased cookie sheet. With your thumb or the blunt handle of a spoon, make an indentation in the center of each dough ball.

Place a cherry in the indentation and press down firmly.

In small saucepan, combine chocolate chips, condensed milk and cherry juice. Stir constantly over low heat until chocolate is melted and mixture is smooth.

Place a teaspoonful or so of chocolate mixture on top of each cherry and smooth over cookie surface.

Bake for 10 minutes. Remove from oven and let cookies cool on cookie sheet for 1 minute, then transfer to cooling rack. (Makes 3 to 4 dozen.)

To drain the cherries, place them on a paper towel for a few minutes and then pat each one dry before placing it on the cookie.

Basic Cookie Dough Recipe on Page 7

Chocolate Fudge Thumbprints

These are one of my all-time favorites! The fudge filling in the middle is smooth and rich and the chocolate chip cookie base is crispy and delicious. This truly is one of those easy cookies that looks like you spend twice as much time making it as you actually do. Try this when you need an extra-special cookie for an extra-special occasion! (Or just to have at home when you're in the mood for a chocolately treat.)

For a little change in flavor, roll the dough in egg whites to coat, then in $1/2$ cup ground hazelnuts instead of the sugar.

     1 recipe Basic Cookie Dough
     2 tablespoons half-and-half or milk
     $1/2$ cup mini-chocolate chips
     2 tablespoons sugar

Preheat oven to 375°. In medium bowl, combine half-and-half with Basic Cookie Dough and beat until blended. Stir in chocolate chips.

Roll dough into balls about 1 $1/2$ inches wide. Roll balls in sugar to coat and place 2 inches apart on ungreased cookie sheet.

With your thumb or blunt handle of a spoon, make an indentation in the center of each dough ball. Bake for 10 minutes. Remove from oven. If the indentation isn't very apparent, take the back of a spoon and press the center of each cookie to make a small "well."

Make fudge filling and drop about a teaspoonful into each indentation. (Makes 3 $1/2$ to 4 dozen.)

Fudge Filling

$^3/_4$ cup semi-sweet chocolate chips
1 tablespoon shortening
2 tablespoons corn syrup
1 tablespoon water
1 teaspoon vanilla extract

Combine chocolate chips and shortening in a small saucepan. Cook over very low heat, stirring constantly until chocolate is melted and mixture is smooth.

Remove from heat and stir in corn syrup, water and vanilla.

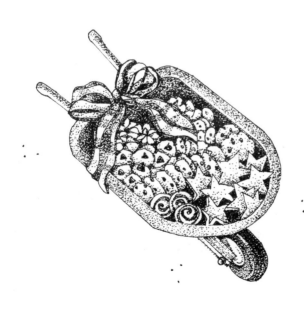

Basic Cookie Dough Recipe on Page 7

37

Peanut Butter and Chocolate Kisses

Who can resist the flavor of chocolate and peanut butter combined? This cookie is a snap to make and a big favorite. Consider making the dough ahead of time and refrigerating until you're ready to bake the cookies. You'll save loads of time and have a fresh batch of cookies ready in minutes.

♥ ♥ ♥

1 recipe Basic Cookie Dough
$^1/_2$ cup peanut butter
3 tablespoons sugar
36-42 chocolate kisses candies

Preheat oven to 375°. In medium bowl combine Basic Cookie Dough with peanut butter. Blend well.

Place sugar in a shallow dish or bowl.

Shape dough into balls 1 $^1/_2$ inches in diameter and roll in sugar. Place 2 inches apart on ungreased cookie sheet and using your thumb or rounded handle of a spoon, make a small indentation in the top of each dough ball.

Bake for 5 minutes. Remove from oven and immediately place a chocolate kiss in each indentation, pressing down gently but firmly.

Place back in the oven and bake for another 3 minutes. Remove from oven and let cookies cool on cookie sheet for 1 minute before transferring to cooling rack. (Makes 3 to 3 $^1/_2$ dozen.)

Tropical Thumbprint Cookies

These delicious citrus cookies keep very well.

    1 recipe Basic Cookie Dough
    2 tablespoons lemon zest
    1 egg white
    1 cup coconut
    $1/2$ cup pineapple jam

Preheat oven to 375°. In medium bowl, add lemon zest to Basic Cookie Dough and beat until well blended. Take heaping teaspoonfuls of dough and roll into $1^1/_2$-inch balls. Dip each dough ball into egg white, then roll in coconut to coat.

Place 3 inches apart on lightly greased cookie sheet. With rounded, blunt spoon handle or your thumb, make an indentation in center of each dough ball.

Fill with about $1/_3$ teaspoonful pineapple jam.

Bake for 11 to 13 minutes or until lightly browned. Remove from oven and let cool for 1 minute before transferring to cooling rack. (Makes 3 to 3 $1/_2$ dozen.)

Basic Cookie Dough Recipe on Page 7

Chocolate Almond Fingers

Tasty little finger-shaped chocolate cookies loaded with almond flavor, dipped in dark chocolate and rolled in almonds.

1 recipe Basic Cookie Dough
2 (1 ounce) squares unsweetened chocolate, melted
2 tablespoons half-and-half
$1/2$ teaspoon almond extract
1 cup ground almonds

Preheat oven to 375°. In medium bowl, combine Basic Cookie Dough with chocolate, half-and-half and almond extract. Beat until dough is thoroughly mixed.

Using your hands, take small pieces of dough (about a teaspoonful) and roll into "ropes" about 4-inches long and about $1/2$-inch wide. (If dough is sticky or difficult to roll, refrigerate for an hour or two to chill slightly.)

Place 2 inches apart on ungreased cookie sheet. Bake for 10 minutes. Remove from oven and let cookies cool on cookie sheet for 1 minute, then transfer to cooling rack.

When cool, dip half of each cookie in chocolate glaze, then roll glazed portion in almonds. Place on wax paper to set. Once set, cookies can be stored in single layers with wax paper between them. (Makes 3 to 3 $1/2$ dozen.)

Chocolate Glaze

1 cup semi-sweet chocolate chips
2 tablespoons shortening

Combine chocolate chips and shortening in small saucepan over low heat. Stir constantly until chocolate is melted and mixture is smooth. Remove from heat.

Chocolate Thumbprints

It may simply be personal preference, but I think these taste especially good with the blackberry jam!

1 recipe Basic Cookie Dough
$^1/_2$ teaspoon almond extract
$^1/_2$ cup cocoa powder
4 tablespoons milk
$^1/_4$ cup sugar
$^1/_4$ cup raspberry, cherry or seedless blackberry jam

Preheat oven to 375°. In medium bowl, mix almond extract, cocoa powder and milk with Basic Cookie Dough until completely blended.

Place sugar in shallow bowl.

Take heaping teaspoonfuls of dough and roll into balls about 1 $^1/_2$ inches wide. Roll balls in sugar to coat.

Place on lightly greased cookie sheet. With blunt handle of a spoon or your thumb, make an indentation in the top of each dough ball. Fill with $^1/_3$ teaspoon jam.

Bake for 10 minutes. Remove from oven and let cookies cool on cookie sheet for 1 minute before transferring to cooling rack. (Makes 3 to 3 $^1/_2$ dozen.)

Basic Cookie Dough Recipe on Page 7

Festive Cranberry Cookies

1 recipe Basic Cookie Dough
$^1/_2$ cup shortening
1 tablespoon orange zest (grated orange rind)
$^2/_3$ cup chopped dried sweetened cranberries
4 drops red food coloring
$^1/_2$ cup finely chopped walnuts or pecans

In medium bowl, blend Basic Cookie Dough with shortening until mixture is smooth. Remove one third of dough and place in small bowl. Add orange zest to this third and beat until well mixed.

Add cranberries and red food coloring to remaining two thirds of dough and beat until dough is evenly colored. Stir in walnuts. Divide dough in half.

Line the bottom of a 9 x 5 (or 8 x 4)-inch loaf pan with plastic wrap or waxed paper. Press half the cranberry dough in the bottom of the loaf pan. Place orange dough evenly on top and press down firmly. Press the remaining half of the cranberry dough evenly over orange dough and press down.

Cover and refrigerate for several hours. When firm, invert pan and peel plastic wrap or waxed paper from dough. Using sharp knife, cut dough into thirds. Slice each third crosswise into $^1/_4$-inch slices and place on ungreased cookie sheet.

Preheat oven to 375°. Bake cookies for 10 minutes or until edges are lightly browned. Remove from oven and let cookies cool on cookie sheet for 1 minute, then transfer to cooling rack. (Makes 3 dozen.)

Peppermint Candy Cane Cookies

These get rave reviews from my 14-year-old, Clayton. "Mom, these are good!" are some of the most satisfying words you'll hear from a teenage son. These red and white cookies shaped like candy canes are very easy to make. If you have the dough ready in the fridge, they take a few minutes to put together and can be a lot of fun for anyone who likes to play with dough.

♥ ♥ ♥

1 recipe Basic Cookie Dough
1 teaspoon peppermint extract
Several drops red food coloring

Preheat oven to 375°. Mix peppermint extract into Basic Cookie Dough.

Divide dough in half. Color one half red with a few drops of red food coloring.

Take a teaspoonful of red dough and roll into a rope about 6-inches long. Take a teaspoonful of the uncolored dough and roll into a rope the same length. Put the two pieces next to each other, and gently twist. (I generally lift one end and twist toward the middle. I then lift and twist the other end as I place it on the cookie sheet.)

Place on ungreased cookie sheet, shaping the top half of the dough into a crook shape (like a candy cane). Bake for 10 minutes and remove from oven. Let cookies cool on cookie sheet for 1 minute, then transfer to cooling rack. To keep their pretty colors, try not to let them brown too much. (Makes about 1 ½ to 2 dozen.)

Basic Cookie Dough Recipe on Page 7

43

Chocolate Striped Cookies

These rectangular chocolate cookies have orderly little stripes--alternating ribbons of chocolate and chocolate-chip flavored dough. They are a big hit at my house. No one can resist chocolate chip cookies and these crisp ones are no exception. They're fun to make too and can be ready at a moment's notice. Simply prepare them ahead of time and refrigerate. You can have fresh, hot cookies in a matter of minutes.

1 recipe Basic Cookie Dough
$1/2$ cup shortening
1 teaspoon rum flavoring
$1/3$ cup chocolate chips, melted
$1/2$ cup chopped nuts
$1/3$ cup miniature chocolate chips

Blend Basic Cookie Dough with shortening until mixture is smooth. Divide dough in half.

Add rum flavoring and melted chocolate to one half and blend well. Stir in nuts. Divide dough in half and set aside.

Add chocolate chips to remaining half and mix well. Divide dough in half.

Line the bottom of a 9 x 5 (or 8 x 4)-inch loaf pan with plastic wrap or waxed paper. Press half of chocolate mixture in the bottom of the loaf pan. Press one half of chocolate chip dough on top and press down firmly.

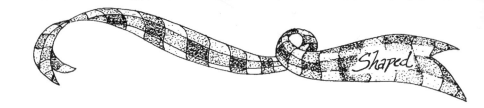

Press the remaining half of the chocolate dough on top and press down . Top with remaining chocolate chip dough and press down firmly.

Cover and refrigerate for several hours. When firm, invert pan and peel plastic wrap or waxed paper from dough. Using sharp knife, cut dough into thirds, each piece will be about 3 inches wide. Slice each third crosswise into $1/4$-inch slices and place on ungreased cookie sheet.

Preheat oven to 375°. Bake cookies for 10 minutes or until edges are lightly browned. Remove from oven and let cool on cookie sheet for 1 minute, then transfer to cooling rack. (Makes 3 dozen.)

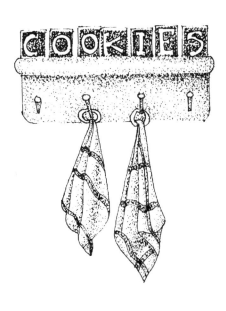

Basic Cookie Dough Recipe on Page 7

45

Spicy Cinnamon Sugar Twists

1 recipe Basic Cookie Dough
$^1/_4$ teaspoon ground nutmeg
2 teaspoons cinnamon, divided
2 pinches ground cloves
$^1/_2$ cup sugar

Preheat oven to 375°. In large bowl, add nutmeg, 1 teaspoon cinnamon and cloves to Basic Cookie Dough. Beat until well mixed.

Using your hands, roll heaping tablespoonfuls of dough into ropes 6-inches long. Fold in half and twist two times.

Place on ungreased cookie sheet.
Bake for 7 minutes or until edges are
lightly browned.

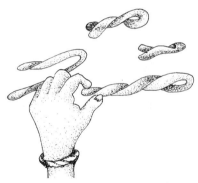

While cookies are baking, combine
remaining cinnamon and sugar in
small bowl and transfer to shallow
dish. Set aside.

Remove cookies from oven and let them remain on cookie sheet for 1 minute, then transfer to cooling rack. When slightly cooled, roll cookies gently in cinnamon and sugar mixture. (Makes 3 to 3 $^1/_2$ dozen.)

Heavenly Holiday Rounds

1 recipe Basic Cookie Dough
2 teaspoons rum flavoring
$^1/_8$ teaspoon ground nutmeg
$^2/_3$ cup finely chopped candied cherries
$^1/_2$ cup coconut

In medium bowl, mix rum flavoring and nutmeg into Basic Cookie Dough until thoroughly blended. Stir in cherries.

Divide dough in half. Form each half into a log about 2 inches in diameter. Roll each log in coconut to cover entirely.

Wrap in plastic wrap and refrigerate for several hours.

When ready to bake, set oven temperature to 375°. Cut $^1/_4$-inch slices from each log and place 2 inches apart on ungreased cookie sheet. Bake for 8 to 10 minutes or until very lightly browned around edges. (Makes 3 to 3 $^1/_2$ dozen.)

Basic Cookie Dough Recipe on Page 7

Chocolate Mint Thins

These crispy, mint-flavored chocolate glazed treats are similar to the Girl Scout cookies so many people know and love!

♥ ♥ ♥

1 recipe Basic Cookie Dough
2 (1 ounce) squares unsweetened
   chocolate, melted

2 tablespoons half-and-half
1 teaspoon peppermint extract

In medium bowl, combine Basic Cookie Dough with chocolate, half-and-half and peppermint extract. Beat until dough is thoroughly mixed.

Divide dough in half and roll each half into a log about 2 inches in diameter. Wrap each dough roll carefully in plastic wrap or wax paper and refrigerate for several hours or overnight.

Preheat oven to 375°. Slice each dough roll into pieces $1/8$-inch thick and place 2 inches apart on ungreased cookie sheet. Bake for 7 minutes. Remove from oven and let cookies cool on cookie sheet for 1 minute, then transfer to cooling rack.

When cool, dip each cookie in chocolate coating using fork to lower them into coating and lift them out. Let excess coating drip off. Place on a piece of wax paper to set chocolate coating. Once chocolate is set, cookies can be stored in an airtight container with sheets of wax paper between the layers. (Makes $4 1/2$ to 5 dozen.)

Chocolate Coating

1 (20 ounce) package chocolate coating
   used for candy-making
6 tablespoons shortening

In small saucepan over very low heat, combine chocolate coating and shortening. Stir constantly until chocolate is melted and mixture is smooth. (Be careful not to cook on medium or higher temperature, because the mixture may harden.) Remove from heat.

Orange Slices

1 recipe Basic Cookie Dough
1 tablespoon orange zest (grated orange rind)
1 teaspoon cinnamon
$^1/_2$ cup ground walnuts

In medium bowl, blend beat orange zest and cinnamon into Basic Cookie Dough until well mixed.

Divide dough in half and form each half into a log about 2 inches in diameter.

Roll each log in ground walnuts to cover completely.

Wrap in plastic wrap and refrigerate several hours or until firm.

When ready to bake, preheat oven to 375°. Slice each log into pieces $^1/_4$-inch thick. Place dough slices on ungreased cookie sheet and bake for 8 to 10 minutes or until cookies are lightly browned around edges.

Remove from oven and let cookies cool on cookie sheet for 1 minute before transferring to cooling rack. (Makes 3 to 3 $^1/_2$ dozen.)

Basic Cookie Dough Recipe on Page 7

Lemon Anise Rounds

1 recipe Basic Cookie Dough
1 teaspoon anise seed
1 teaspoon anise extract
$^1/_2$ teaspoon lemon extract

In medium bowl, mix anise seed, anise extract and lemon extract into Basic Cookie Dough until thoroughly combined.

Divide dough in half. Form each half into a log about 2 inches in diameter. Wrap in plastic wrap and refrigerate for several hours or until firm.

When ready to bake, preheat oven to 375°. Slice each log into pieces $^1/_4$-inch thick. Place cookies on ungreased cookie sheet and bake for 10 to 12 minutes or until edges are lightly browned.

Remove from oven and let cookies cool on cookie sheet for 1 minute, then transfer to cooling rack. (Makes 3 to 3 $^1/_2$ dozen.)

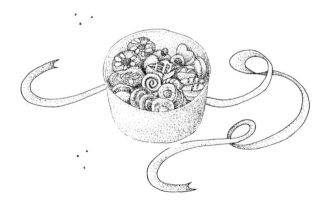

Snappy Peanut Butter Cookies

1 recipe Basic Cookie Dough
1 cup peanut butter, smooth or crunchy
$^1/_4$ cup sugar

Preheat oven to 375°. In medium bowl, add peanut butter to Basic Cookie Dough and mix well.

Roll heaping teaspoonfuls of dough into balls and roll in sugar to coat. Place 3 inches apart on ungreased cookie sheet. Make crisscross pattern with fork on top of cookies to flatten.

Bake for 10 minutes. Remove from oven and let cookies cool for 1 minute on cookie sheet before transferring to cooling rack. (Makes 3 to 3 $^1/_2$ dozen.)

Basic Cookie Dough Recipe on Page 7

51

Raisin Gingersnaps

1 recipe Basic Cookie Dough
1 teaspoon baking soda
1/4 cup molasses
1 teaspoon ground ginger
1/4 teaspoon ground cloves
1 cup raisins
1/4 cup sugar

Preheat oven to 375°. In medium bowl, mix baking soda, molasses, ginger and cloves into Basic Cookie Dough until thoroughly blended. Stir in raisins.

Take heaping teaspoonfuls of dough and roll into balls. Roll balls in sugar and place 2 inches apart on lightly greased cookie sheet.

Bake for 10 minutes. Let cookies cool on cookie sheet for 1 minute before transferring to cooling rack. (Makes 3 to 3 1/2 dozen.)

Chocolate-Covered Mocha Balls

Chocolate is so hard to resist. These little cookies look simply delectable. The chocolate coating over these perfectly round, mocha-flavored cookies makes them a star of the dessert table. For a really dramatic effect, top them with silver or gold candy decorations while the coating is still wet.

    1 recipe Basic Cookie Dough
    4 tablespoons shortening, divided
    1 1/2 teaspoons cinnamon
    2 tablespoons instant coffee
    5 ounces chocolate coating for candy making

Preheat oven to 375°. In large bowl, combine Basic Cookie Dough with 2 tablespoons shortening, cinnamon and instant coffee.

Roll dough into balls 1 1/2 inches in diameter and place 2 inches apart on ungreased cookie sheet.

Bake for 10 minutes, then remove from oven and let cool on cookie sheet for 1 minute. Transfer to cooling rack.

When cool, melt chocolate coating with remaining 2 tablespoons shortening over very low heat, stirring constantly.

Using a fork, lift each cookie ball from underneath (don't skewer them), and then dip in the melted chocolate coating. Place dipped cookies on wax paper until chocolate coating sets, then store in covered container. (Makes 4 to 4 1/2 dozen.)

Basic Cookie Dough Recipe on Page 7

Chocolate Dipped Malted Milk Rounds

These delightful crispy cookies have the flavor of malted milk ball candy. The crunchy cookie is loaded with malted milk flavor and the chocolate coating tops it off. They're easy to make and sharp looking! By shaping the dough into balls, the cookies bake perfectly round. And the chocolate coating over half the cookie looks very stylish.

1 recipe Basic Cookie Dough
$1/2$ cup shortening
$1/4$ cup packed brown sugar
1 cup malted milk powder

Preheat oven to 375°. In large bowl, combine Basic Cookie Dough with shortening; blend well. Beat in brown sugar and malted milk powder.

Roll dough into balls 1 $1/2$-inches wide and place 3 inches apart on ungreased cookie sheet. Bake for 10 to 12 minutes until edges are brown.

Remove from oven and let cookies cool on cookie sheet for 1 minute, then transfer to cooling rack.

When cool, dip half of each cookie in chocolate coating, shake excess coating off and place on wax paper to set. (To do this, I find it's easiest to hold the pan with one hand, tilting it so the chocolate pools in the bottom and use my other hand to dip the cookies. I also gently scrape the back of the cookie against the pan's side to remove excess chocolate from the back.)

When chocolate is set, store cookies with a layer of wax paper between them.

Chocolate Coating

10 ounces chocolate-flavored candy coating (like you
    would use to make almond bark*)
1 tablespoon shortening

In small saucepan, melt chocolate and shortening over very low
heat, stirring constantly. When mixture is smooth, remove from
heat.

*You can also use 1 ¹/₂ cups milk chocolate chips in place of the
chocolate candy coating if you can't locate it. I like the
chocolate coating because it sets very quickly and the cookies
can be immediately stored.

Basic Cookie Dough Recipe on Page 7

Nutty Lemon Rounds

1 recipe Basic Cookie Dough
3 tablespoons lemon juice
2 teaspoons lemon zest (grated lemon rind)
$^1/_2$ cup coconut
$^1/_2$ cup finely chopped pecans
2 tablespoons sugar

Preheat oven to 375°. In medium bowl, combine Basic Cookie Dough with lemon juice and lemon zest. Beat until well blended.

Stir in coconut and pecans.

Roll dough into balls about 1 $^1/_2$-inches wide and place 2 inches apart on ungreased cookie sheet. Gently flatten with the lightly-greased bottom of a glass dipped in sugar.

Bake for 9 to 11 minutes, just until edges begin to brown. Remove from oven and let cookies cool on cookie sheet for 1 minute, then transfer to cooling rack. (Makes 4 $^1/_2$ to 5 dozen.)

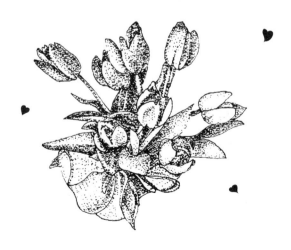

Cherry Caps

What an easy, colorful cookie to lend a holiday touch to your dessert table. For a really festive appearance, make half with green cherries and half with red cherries. If you have the dough made ahead of time, you can make these in minutes and have fresh, warm cookies in a snap.

1 recipe Basic Cookie Dough
$1/2$ teaspoon almond extract
18-21 candied cherries, halved

Preheat oven to 375°. In medium bowl, combine Basic Cookie Dough with almond extract and beat until thoroughly blended.

Roll pieces of dough into 1-inch balls and place 2 inches apart on ungreased cookie sheet. Top each dough ball with a cherry half, cut side down.

Bake for 10 minutes, then remove from oven and let cookies cool on cookie sheet for 1 minute. Transfer to cooling rack. (Makes 3 to 3 $1/2$ dozen.)

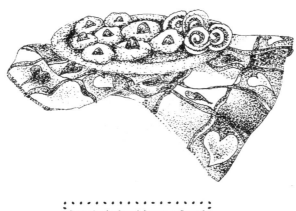

Basic Cookie Dough Recipe on Page 7

Chocolate Chip Hazelnut Mounds

These light, delicate cookies are loaded with hazelnut flavor and studded with chocolate chips.

        1 recipe Basic Cookie Dough
        ¹/₄ cup shortening
        1 cup mini-chocolate chips
        1 cup ground hazelnuts
        ¹/₄ cup sifted powdered sugar

Preheat oven to 350°. In medium bowl, combine Basic Cookie Dough with shortening and beat until well blended.

Stir in chocolate chips and hazelnuts.

Roll dough into 1-inch balls and place 2 inches apart on ungreased cookie sheet.

Bake for 15 to 18 minutes or until edges just begin to brown. Remove from oven and let cookies cool on cookie sheet for 1 minute, then transfer to cooling rack. When cool, dip cookies in powdered sugar to coat. (Makes 3 ¹/₂ to 4 dozen.)

Molasses Rounds

1 recipe Basic Cookie Dough
1 $1/2$ teaspoons cinnamon, divided
1 teaspoon ground ginger
$1/2$ cup molasses
$1/2$ cup packed brown sugar
2 tablespoons sugar

Preheat oven to 375°. In medium bowl, combine Basic Cookie
Dough with 1 teaspoon cinnamon, ginger, molasses and brown
sugar. Beat until dough is well blended.

Roll dough into balls about 1 $1/2$-inches wide. Place 2 inches apart
on ungreased cookie sheet.

In small shallow bowl, combine remaining cinnamon
and sugar. Stir until well mixed.

Grease bottom of a glass and dip in
sugar, then use to flatten each cookie,
dipping glass back in the sugar-
cinnamon mixture before flattening next
cookie.

Bake for 8 to 10 minutes. Remove from oven and let cookies cool
on cookie sheet for 1 minute, then transfer to cooling rack.
(Makes 4 dozen.)

Basic Cookie Dough Recipe on Page 7

Stained Glass Shapes

When baked, these colorful cookies have see-through candy "windows" that look like colored glass. You can use a combination of colors and shapes. Don't restrict yourself to cutting out only one area from the center of the cookie. You can find small cookie cutters (or even a thimble will work) and cut several areas, then fill them with different colors of candy. Try this at Easter time using an egg-shaped cookie and pastel candy colors.

The amount of crushed candy you need will vary somewhat depending on what sizes your cookie cutters are and how many colors you want to use. You can start with a small amount and then crush additional candies as you need them. A little bit goes a long way.

♥ ❤ ♥

1 recipe Basic Cookie Dough, chilled
$^1/_4$–$^1/_3$ cup crushed hard candies*

Preheat oven to 350°. Divide dough in half, keeping half not used in refrigerator. Roll dough out to $^1/_8$-inch thickness. Cut shapes with cookie cutter, then cut smaller design out of center, taking care to leave a $^1/_2$ inch to $^3/_4$-inch dough border.

Place cut-out cookie carefully on cookie sheet covered with foil. Fill cut-out center with crushed candy. The amount needed will vary depending upon the size of the cut-out area. Try to keep the candy in the cut-out area and not get it on the cookie itself or you'll end up coloring the dough.

Bake for 10 to 12 minutes. Remove from oven and let cookies cool completely, then gently remove cookies from foil by peeling the foil away from them.

*Crush the hard candy by putting it in a resealable plastic bag and pounding it gently with a mallet.

Basic Cookie Dough Recipe on Page 7

Rolled

Anise Cut-Outs

If you like the taste of licorice, you'll like these cookies. They are crispy and light with a hint of licorice.

     1 recipe Basic Cookie Dough
     1 teaspoon anise seed
     1 teaspoon anise extract
     $^1/_4$ cup sugar
     $^1/_2$ teaspoon cinnamon

Preheat oven to 350°. In medium bowl, add anise seeds and anise extract to Basic Cookie Dough. Beat until well blended.

In small bowl, combine sugar and cinnamon and mix well.

Roll dough out on lightly floured surface to $^1/_8$-inch thickness. Either cut into squares with sharp knife or cut out shapes with cookie cutter.

Place cookies on lightly greased cookie sheet and sprinkle a little of the cinnamon and sugar mixture over each.

Bake for 10 minutes. Remove from oven and let cookies cool on cookie sheet for 1 minute before transferring to cooling rack. (Makes 3 to 3 $^1/_2$ dozen.)

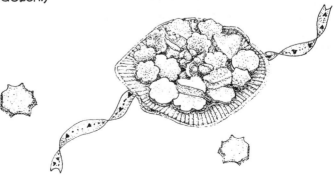

Strawberry Delights

These colorful, pretty cookies are easy to make and look extra special.

1 recipe Basic Cookie Dough, chilled
1 cup strawberry filling (approximately a 12 ounce can)
$^1/_2$ cup ground almonds

Preheat oven to 375°. Divide Basic Cookie Dough in half and roll out one half at a time, keeping other half refrigerated until ready to use.

Roll dough to $^1/_4$-inch thickness on a well-floured surface. Cut out cookie circles with 2 inch or 2 $^1/_2$-inch diameter biscuit cutter or round cookie cutter.

Place cookies 2 inches apart on ungreased cookie. Spread about $^3/_4$ teaspoonful of filling in center of each cookie and sprinkle almonds over top. Carefully bring edge of one side of cookie to middle of cookie. Fold the other side in the same way, overlapping the first edge slightly.

Bake for 10 minutes or until edges are lightly browned. Remove from oven and let cookies cool on cookie sheet for 1 minute before transferring to cooling rack. (Makes 3 to 3 $^1/_2$ dozen.)

Basic Cookie Dough Recipe on Page 7

Date-Filled Half-Moons

These little puffy crescent-shaped cookies are stuffed with a rich and flavorful filling. Although they'd be great any time of the year, they are especially nice around Thanksgiving and go really well with the other seasonal flavors.

1 recipe Basic Cookie Dough
1 tablespoon orange zest (grated orange rind)
$3/4$ cup packed brown sugar
1 tablespoon flour
Pinch salt
$1/2$ cup water
$1/2$ cup chopped dates
$1/2$ teaspoon cinnamon
1 cup finely chopped walnuts

Mix Basic Cookie Dough with orange zest until thoroughly blended and chill for several hours or overnight.

Prepare filling. Combine brown sugar, flour, salt, water, dates and cinnamon in medium saucepan and bring to a boil. Cook for 4 minutes, stirring frequently, until mixture is thickened. (While mixture is cooking, try to mash the dates using the back of a spoon or a potato masher.)

Remove from heat and let cool to lukewarm. Stir in nuts.

Preheat oven to 375°. Divide dough in half and work with one half at a time. Roll dough out into a circle $1/8$-inch thick. Cut circles using 2 $1/2$ inch or 3-inch round cookie cutter. Place dough circles 1 inch apart on lightly greased cookie sheet.

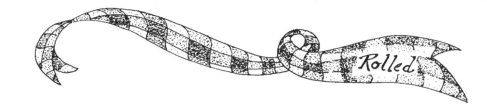

Place scant teaspoon of filling on one half of each dough circle, keeping it $1/4$ inch from the edge of the dough round. (The amount of filling you use will vary depending on the size of the dough circles you cut. You may need to adjust the filling slightly so you have the right amount for the size of the cookie you're making.)

Gently lift the half of the dough circle without filling and lap it over the half with the filling, keeping edges even. Crimp edges closed using tip of a fork and prick the top of the cookie before baking.

Bake for 8 to 10 minutes, just until edges begin to brown. Remove from oven and let cool for 1 minute, then transfer to cooling rack. (Makes 3 to 3 $1/2$ dozen.)

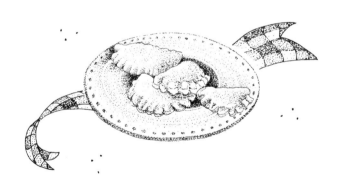

Basic Cookie Dough Recipe on Page 7

Cherry "Turnovers"

1 recipe Basic Cookie Dough, chilled
1 cup cherry pie filling, with cherries mashed*

½ cup powdered sugar
¼ teaspoon almond extract
2 teaspoons warm water

Preheat oven to 375°. Divide dough in half, keeping one half refrigerated while you roll the other half into a circle ⅛-inch thick.

Using a 2 ½ inch or 3-inch round cookie cutter, cut circles of dough, placing half the circles on lightly greased cookie sheet.

*To mash the cherries in the pie filling, I put the filling in a small bowl or measuring cup and then use a fork to mash them. The whole cherries are much too large for a small cookie like this.

Place a scant teaspoon of filling on one half of each dough round on the cookie sheet, taking care to keep filling ¼ inch from the border. (You'll need to adjust the amount of filling to the size of the rounds. If you're using a 2 ½-inch cookie cutter, you'll need to use about a half teaspoon of filling.)

Gently lift the side of dough without filling to cover the side with filling, aligning edges of dough. Crimp the edges with a fork to seal them.

Remove from oven and let cookies cool on cookie sheet for 1 minute, then transfer to cooling rack. (Makes 3 to 3 ½ dozen.)

When cool, drizzle with glaze. To make the glaze, combine the powdered sugar, almond extract and water in a small bowl or measuring cup. Mix well.

Use a spoon to scoop up the glaze and then drizzle in a fine stream over the cookies or place the glaze in a small plastic bag, like a sandwich bag. Twist the bag above the glaze and snip the corner. You can get better control this way by using just enough pressure to keep a steady stream of glaze coming out.

Apricot-Filled Treats

These are very similar to the "Mincemeat Pies." Both complement each other wonderfully and look great when served together on a large platter.

♥ ♥ ♥

2 tablespoons sugar
$^1/_8$ teaspoon cinnamon
Pinch of ground nutmeg
1 recipe Basic Cookie Dough, chilled
$^1/_2$-$^3/_4$ cup apricot preserves

Preheat oven to 375°. In small bowl, combine the sugar, cinnamon and nutmeg. Stir until well mixed. Set aside.

Roll Basic Cookie Dough to $^1/_8$-inch thickness. Cut out rounds using 2 $^1/_2$-inch or 3-inch cookie cutter. Place half the rounds 2 inches apart on lightly greased cookie sheet.

Place a teaspoon of preserves in the center of each round, then place another round on top.

Crimp the edges using the tip of a fork to seal them. Sprinkle a little of the sugar mixture over each cookie and bake for 10 to 12 minutes.

Remove from oven and let cookies cool on cookie sheet for 1 minute, then transfer to cooling rack. (Makes about 2 dozen.)

Basic Cookie Dough Recipe on Page 7

67

Apple Pie Bites

These fantastic little cookies taste *just* like apple pie, but can be eaten without a fork. These adorable little bite-sized half-moons filled with apple pie spices and flavor are also *much* easier to make than an apple pie.

Be sure and serve these soon after they're baked because the filling has a lot of moisture and the cookie absorbs it and can become very soft. It's best to store them in a single layer in a loosely-covered container.

> 1 recipe Basic Cookie Dough, chilled
> $1/2$ teaspoon, plus $1/8$ teaspoon cinnamon
> 2 tablespoons sugar
> 1 cup apple pie filling, with apples finely chopped*

Mix $1/2$ teaspoon cinnamon into Basic Cookie Dough. Chill.

In small bowl, combine sugar and remaining $1/8$ teaspoon cinnamon. Mix well and set aside.

Preheat oven to 375°. Divide dough in half, keeping one half refrigerated while you roll the other half into a circle $1/8$-inch thick.

Using a 2 $1/2$ inch or 3-inch round cookie cutter, cut circles of dough, placing half the circles on lightly greased cookie sheet.

*To chop the large pieces of apple in the pie filling, I place the filling in a small bowl or measuring cup and then use a sharp knife to slice it into finer pieces. The filling usually comes with apple slices that are too large for a small cookie like this.

68

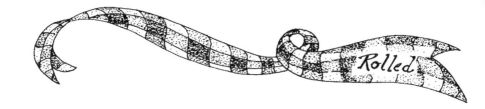

Place a scant teaspoon of filling on one half of each dough round on the cookie sheet, taking care to keep filling $1/4$ inch from the border. (You'll need to adjust the amount of filling you use to the size of the rounds you're using. If you're using a $2 \, 1/2$-inch cookie cutter, you'll need to use about a half teaspoon of filling.)

Gently lift the side of dough without filling to cover the side with filling, aligning edges of dough. Crimp the edges with a fork to seal them.

Sprinkle each cookie with a little of the sugar and cinnamon mixture, then bake for 8 to 10 minutes, until edges are lightly brown.

Remove from oven and let cookies cool on cookie sheet for 1 minute, then transfer to cooling rack. (Makes 3 to $3 \, 1/2$ dozen.)

Basic Cookie Dough Recipe on Page 7

69

Rugalach

This cookie version of a bakery favorite combines the flavor of nuts, jam and cinnamon into a tasty little treat that tastes a lot like the real thing. They're easy to make and full of flavor. You can vary the flavor by choosing different flavor preserves. I frequently make half the batch with raspberry and half with apricot for a little variety.

♥ ♥ ♥

1 tablespoon sugar
1/4 teaspoon cinnamon
1 recipe Basic Cookie Dough, chilled
3/4 cup raspberry, blackberry
   or cherry preserves

1/2 cup ground pecans
   or walnuts
1/2 cup raisins
1 egg, slightly beaten

Preheat oven to 375°. Combine sugar and cinnamon in small bowl and mix well. Set aside.

Divide dough in half and roll out one half at a time, keeping other half refrigerated until ready to use. Roll dough out on well-floured surface into circle about 1/4-inch thick.

Spread half the preserves evenly over the surface. Sprinkle half the nuts evenly over preserves. Sprinkle half the raisins evenly on top.

Using sharp knife, cut circle into 16 wedges. Starting at the wide end of each wedge, carefully roll the dough. (You'll end up with a crescent shape.)

Place 3 inches apart on lightly greased cookie sheet. Using pastry brush, brush egg lightly over surface, then sprinkle a little of the cinnamon-sugar mixture over each. Repeat with remaining half of Basic Cookie Dough and ingredients.

Bake for 15 to 18 minutes, until edges are nicely browned. Remove from oven and immediately transfer cookies to cooling rack. (Makes about 3 1/2 dozen.)

Mincemeat "Pies"

These are cute little things! Essentially little bite size pies, these round, pillow-shaped treats are a lot easier to serve and eat. The egg-wash brushed over them before they are baked gives them a nice shiny finish.

❤ ❤ ❤

1 recipe Basic Cookie Dough, chilled
$^1/_3$ cup mincemeat filling*
1 egg, slightly beaten

Preheat oven to 375°. Divide chilled Basic Cookie Dough in half and keep one half in the refrigerator while you roll the other half out to $^1/_8$-inch thickness.

Using a 2 $^1/_2$ inch or 3-inch round cookie cutter, cut circles of dough and place half of them 2 inches apart on lightly greased cookie sheets.

Place a teaspoon of mincemeat filling in the center of each dough round on the cookie sheet, and then place another dough round on top. Crimp the edges of the cookies by using the tip of a fork to press the seams together.

Then, with a pastry brush, put a thin layer of egg over each cookie. Bake for 8 to 10 minutes, until edges are lightly browned.

Remove from oven and let cookies cool on cookie sheet for 1 minute before transferring to cooling rack.
(Makes about 2 dozen.)

***U**se any mincemeat pie filling from a jar or can.

Basic Cookie Dough Recipe on Page 7

71

Pecan Whirls

This is a fast little cookie, but one that looks like you spent a lot of time making it. If you make your dough ahead of time, you simply open a can of filling, make the cookies, chill, then slice and bake.

1 recipe Basic Cookie Dough, chilled
1 cup pecan filling*

Divide Basic Cookie Dough in half, keeping one half refrigerated while you roll out the other half into a 9 x 13-inch rectangle.

Carefully spread the pecan filling evenly over the dough, extending it to within $1/4$ inch of the edges on the short ends.

Starting with short end, roll dough jellyroll fashion. Wrap in plastic wrap or wax paper (taking care to keep dough roll from bending) and chill for several hours. Repeat with other half of Basic Cookie Dough.

Preheat oven to 375°. Unwrap each roll of dough and slice into pieces $1/4$-inch thick. Place pieces flat side down and 2 inches apart on lightly greased cookie sheet.

Bake for 8 to 10 minutes or until edges begin to brown. Remove from oven and let cookies cool on cookie sheet for 1 minute, then transfer to cooling rack. (Makes about 4 dozen.)

*Pecan filling comes in a can.

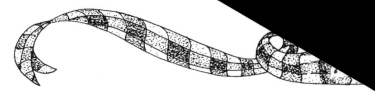

Pineapple Pinwheels

1 recipe Basic Cookie Dough
$^1/_4$ cup shortening
1 tablespoon lemon zest (grated lemon rind)
$^1/_2$ cup pineapple preserves, divided
$^1/_2$ cup ground or finely chopped nuts, divided

In medium bowl, combine Basic Cookie Dough with shortening and lemon zest. Beat until dough is well-blended.

Divide dough in half. On lightly floured surface, roll out one half into a rectangle about 9 x13 inches in diameter. Spread $^1/_4$ cup pineapple preserves evenly over dough. Sprinkle $^1/_4$ cup of nuts evenly over preserves.

Starting with short end, roll dough jellyroll fashion. Repeat with other half of dough.

Wrap each dough roll in plastic and refrigerate for several hours.

Preheat oven to 375°. Slice each roll into pieces $^1/_4$-inch thick and place 2 inches apart on well greased cookie sheet. Bake for 10 minutes, or until edges are brown.

Remove from oven and let cookies cool on cookie sheet for 1 minute, then transfer to cooling rack. (Makes 3 $^1/_2$ to 4 dozen.)

I find it's easiest to roll the dough between two sheets of wax paper. Not only is it less messy but it also ensures the dough doesn't stick to the rolling pin. When I'm ready to wrap dough roll, I simply use the wax paper it's sitting on.

Basic Cookie Dough Recipe on Page 7

73

ɔcolate Spirals

ıc Cookie Dough
ɔ squares unsweetened chocolate, melted,
ɹ slightly

Divide Basic Cookie Dough in half. Place one half in medium-size bowl and add melted chocolate. Beat until chocolate is completely mixed into dough.

Roll out remaining plain half of dough into a rectangle about 8-inches wide and 12-inches long. Roll out chocolate dough to the same dimensions.

Place chocolate dough on top of plain dough and starting with the longest side, roll jellyroll fashion into a log. Wrap dough carefully and chill for an hour or so.

Preheat oven to 375°. Remove wrapping from dough, and with sharp knife, slice into $1/4$-inch pieces. Place cookie slices 2 inches apart on ungreased cookie sheet.

Bake for about 10 minutes, then remove from oven and let cookies cool on cookie sheet for 1 minute. Transfer to cooling rack. (Makes 2 to 2 $1/2$ dozen.)

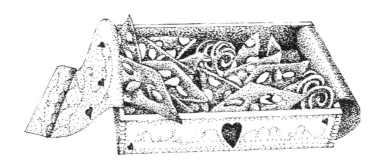

Almond Cherry Pinwheels

This is another one of those recipes I like so much because of the speed with which you can make a snack that looks and tastes fantastic. I like to prepare the dough ahead of time so I can slice and bake them when I'm in the mood for a fresh batch. The spiral shape is intriguing and looks difficult, but is really very easy to do.

1 recipe Basic Cookie Dough
$^1/_4$ cup shortening
$^1/_2$ teaspoon almond extract
$^1/_2$ cup cherry preserves, divided
$^1/_2$ cup ground or finely chopped almonds, divided

In medium bowl, combine Basic Cookie Dough with shortening and almond extract. Beat until dough is well-blended.

Divide dough in half. On lightly floured surface, roll out one half into a 9 x 13-inch rectangle. Spread $^1/_4$ cup cherry preserves evenly over dough. Sprinkle $^1/_4$ cup almonds evenly over preserves.

Starting with short end, roll dough jellyroll fashion.

Repeat with other half of dough.

Wrap each dough roll in plastic and refrigerate for several hours.

Preheat oven to 375°. Slice each roll into pieces $^1/_4$-inch thick and place 2 inches apart on well greased cookie sheet. Bake for 10 minutes or until edges are brown.

Remove from oven and let cookies cool on pan for 1 minute, then transfer to cooling rack. (Makes 3 $^1/_2$ to 4 dozen.)

Basic Cookie Dough Recipe on Page 7

Date Nut Pinwheels

1 cup finely chopped dates
$^1/_2$ cup sugar
$^1/_2$ cup water
1 recipe Basic Cookie Dough, chilled
$^1/_2$ cup ground walnuts

In small saucepan, combine dates, sugar and water. Bring to a simmer and cook, stirring occasionally, over medium heat for 3 to 4 minutes, until mixture is thickened. Remove from heat and let cool to room temperature.

Divide Basic Cookie Dough in half. Roll out one half into a rectangle $^1/_4$-inch thick. Spread half date mixture evenly over dough, bringing it to within $^1/_2$ inch of the edge of dough. Sprinkle half the walnuts evenly over date mixture.

Starting with long side, roll dough jellyroll fashion. Wrap in plastic wrap and chill for a couple of hours. Repeat with other half of dough.

Preheat oven to 375°. Slice dough rolls into $^1/_4$-inch pieces and place 2 inches apart on lightly greased cookie sheet. Bake for 10 to 12 minutes or until lightly browned. Remove from oven and let cookies cool on cookie sheet for 1 minute before transferring to cooling rack. (Makes 3 $^1/_2$ to 4 dozen.)

Ginger Jam Sandwich Cookies

1 recipe Basic Cookie Dough
2 teaspoons ground ginger
$1/2$ teaspoon cinnamon
$1/4$ teaspoon ground cloves
$1/2$ cup strawberry jam

Preheat oven to 350°. In medium bowl, combine ginger, cinnamon and cloves with Basic Cookie Dough, and mix well.

Roll small pieces of dough into balls about $3/4$ inch to 1 inch in diameter. Place 2 inches apart on ungreased cookie sheet. Flatten slightly with bottom of glass dipped in sugar.

Bake for 10 to 12 minutes or until lightly browned around edges.

Remove from oven and let cookies cool on cookie sheet for 1 minute before transferring to cooling rack.

When completely cool, place $1/2$ teaspoonful of jam into center back of one cookie and top with flat side of another cookie. Press lightly to distribute jam to edges.

If you want, take a little powdered sugar and sift it over the cookies. It makes a great finishing touch. (Makes 2 $1/2$ to 3 dozen.)

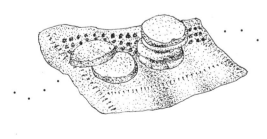

Basic Cookie Dough Recipe on Page 7

Lemon Raisin Sandwich Cookies

If you prefer the flavor of dates, you can replace the raisins in this recipe with them, chopped of course. They'll taste just as good with the citrus flavor of the cookie.

1 recipe Basic Cookie Dough
1 tablespoon lemon juice
1 tablespoon lemon zest (grated lemon rind)
$^2/_3$ cup raisins
3 tablespoons sugar

Preheat oven to 400°. In medium bowl, combine Basic Cookie Dough with lemon juice and lemon zest. Beat well. Stir in raisins.

Form dough into balls 1 $^1/_2$-inches wide. Roll balls in sugar to coat and place 2 inches apart on ungreased cookie sheet. Flatten each with the slightly greased bottom of a glass.

Bake for 8 to 10 minutes, until edges are just lightly browned. Remove from oven and let cookies cool on cookie sheet for 1 minute, then transfer to cooling rack.

When cool, spread flat side of one cookie with generous amount of filling. Place another cookie over filling, flat side down and press together lightly. (Makes 1 $^1/_2$ dozen finished cookies.)

When I make sandwich cookies, I like to give them neat little edges by running the tip of a butter knife between the two cookies after I fill them, turning the cookie as I go, to smooth the filling and even it out.

Filling

1 (8 ounce) package cream cheese, softened
$^1/_2$ cup butter or margarine, softened
$^1/_2$ teaspoon vanilla
4 cups powdered sugar

In small mixing bowl, beat cream cheese and butter until light and fluffy. Beat in vanilla and then powdered sugar a little at a time, beating well after each addition.

Basic Cookie Dough Recipe on Page 7

Jam-Filled Sandwich Cookies

1 recipe Basic Cookie Dough, chilled
$1/3$-$1/2$ cup jam or jelly
Powdered sugar for garnish

Preheat oven to 375°. Divide Basic Cookie Dough in half and work with one half at a time, keeping other half refrigerated until ready to use.

Roll cookie dough out into a circle $1/8$-inch thick. Cut desired shapes with cookie cutter. Take very small cutter and cut a center out of half the cookies. Place cookies 2 inches apart on ungreased cookie sheet.

Bake for 8 to 10 minutes or until cookies are lightly browned around edges.

Remove from oven and let cookies cool on cookie sheet for 1 minute, then transfer to cooling rack.

When cool, place a half teaspoonful of jam on the center back of one solid cookie and spread jam almost to edges. Place a cookie with a cut out center over the jam and press lightly to seal.

Just before serving, dust a little powdered sugar over cookies.

Chocolate Peanut Butter Sandwich Cookies

1 recipe Basic Cookie Dough
2 squares unsweetened chocolate, melted
3 tablespoons sugar

Preheat oven to 350°. In medium bowl add melted chocolate to Basic Cookie Dough and blend well.

Shape dough into 1 ¹/₂-inch balls and place 3 inches apart on ungreased cookie sheet. Use bottom of a glass greased and dipped in sugar to flatten each cookie.

Bake for 10 minutes, then remove from oven. Let cookies cool on cookie sheet for 1 minute before transferring to cooling rack.

When cool, frost flat side of one cookie with about 1 teaspoon of Peanut Butter Filling, and then place flat side of another cookie on top. Press together lightly.

Peanut Butter Filling

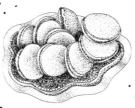

¹/₄ cup creamy peanut butter
1 ¹/₂ cups powdered sugar
2-3 tablespoons milk
¹/₂ teaspoon vanilla

Combine peanut butter, powdered sugar, milk and vanilla in a medium bowl. Beat on medium speed with hand mixer until mixture is smooth and creamy.

Basic Cookie Dough Recipe on Page 7

German Chocolate Sandwich Cookies

1 recipe Basic Cookie Dough
1/4 cup shortening
1/2 cup packed brown sugar
2/3 cup cocoa powder
2 tablespoons milk

Preheat oven to 350°. In large bowl, combine Basic Cookie Dough with shortening, brown sugar, cocoa powder and milk. Beat until thoroughly blended and dough is evenly colored.

Roll pieces of dough into balls 1 1/2-inches wide and place 3 inches apart on ungreased cookie sheet. Take the bottom of a glass (greased with a little shortening or butter) and flatten each dough ball.

Bake for 10 minutes, remove from oven, and let cool cookies cool on cookie sheet for 1 minute. Transfer to cooling rack.

When cool, place about 1 teaspoonful of filling on the back half (flat side) of one cookie, place another cookie (flat side down) on top and press together firmly. (Try to get the filling to the edges of the cookie.) Makes 2 dozen finished cookies.

Warm from the Oven

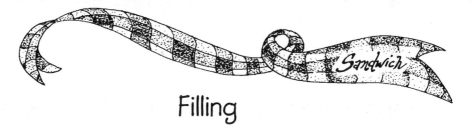

Filling

¹/₂ cup butter or margarine
¹/₂ cup packed brown sugar
¹/₄ cup light corn syrup
1 teaspoon vanilla
1 cup flaked coconut
1 cup finely chopped pecans

Melt butter in a medium saucepan over medium heat. Stir in brown sugar and corn syrup. Bring to a simmer, stirring constantly, and cook for about 3 to 4 minutes, until mixture is thickened.

Remove from heat and stir in vanilla, then coconut and pecans. Use while warm.

Basic Cookie Dough Recipe on Page 7

Spicy Molasses Sandwich Cookies

1 recipe Basic Cookie Dough
$^1/_2$ cup shortening
$^1/_2$ cup molasses
$^1/_2$ teaspoon cinnamon
$^1/_4$ teaspoon ground nutmeg
$^1/_4$ teaspoon ginger
$^1/_4$ teaspoon ground cloves
$^1/_2$ cup quick-cooking oats

Preheat oven to 375°. In large bowl, combine Basic Cookie Dough with shortening, molasses, cinnamon, nutmeg, ginger and cloves. Beat until well mixed. Blend in oats.

Drop by rounded teaspoonful onto ungreased cookie sheet. Bake for 10 minutes. Remove from oven and let cookies cool on cookie sheet 1 minute, then transfer to cooling rack.

When cool, place a teaspoonful of filling on the back side (flat side) of one cookie, then top with flat side of another. Press lightly to force filling to edges of cookie.

Filling

$^3/_4$ cup butter or margarine
2 cups powdered sugar
$^1/_8$ teaspoon salt
1 teaspoon vanilla
1 tablespoon milk
1 (7 ounce) jar marshmallow creme

In medium bowl, cream butter, sugar, salt, vanilla and milk. Add marshmallow creme and beat with hand mixer until mixture is smooth.

Spicy Crumb Cake

1 recipe Basic Cookie Dough
1 teaspoon cinnamon
1 teaspoon ground nutmeg
$^1/_4$ teaspoon allspice
$^1/_4$ teaspoon ground cloves
1 cup buttermilk

$^1/_2$ cup flour
$^1/_2$ cup plus 2 tablespoons sugar
2 tablespoons butter or margarine, softened

Preheat oven to 350°. In large bowl, combine Basic Cookie Dough with cinnamon, nutmeg, allspice, cloves and buttermilk. Beat on medium speed to blend, stopping to scrape bowl as necessary.

Pour batter into greased 9 x 9-inch baking pan.

In small bowl, combine flour and sugar. Cut in butter until mixture is crumbly. Sprinkle over batter in pan.

Bake for 50 minutes to 1 hour or until crumb topping is nicely browned and cake tester comes out clean. Cool and cut into squares.

Basic Cookie Dough Recipe on Page 7

Gingerbread Squares
with Brown Sugar Frosting

Would you believe you can also use the Basic Cookie Dough recipe to create a cake? This easy gingerbread is a modified version of a recipe given to me by my friend, Michele. It's loaded with flavor and as moist as can be. It's great even without the frosting! A little powdered sugar dusted over the cooled cake does the trick.

    1 recipe Basic Cookie Dough
    1/2 cup molasses
    2 teaspoons ginger
    2 teaspoons cinnamon
    1/2 teaspoon ground cloves
    3/4 cup hot black coffee

Preheat oven to 350°. In large bowl, combine Basic Cookie Dough with molasses, ginger, cinnamon and cloves. Beat on low speed, adding coffee a little at a time until the mixture is thoroughly blended.

Pour batter into greased and floured 9-inch square pan.

Bake for 40 minutes or until cake tester comes out clean. Let cool and then frost with Brown Sugar Frosting.

Brown Sugar Frosting

2 tablespoons butter or margarine
2 tablespoons evaporated milk
1/4 cup packed brown sugar
Pinch salt
1/2 teaspoon vanilla
1 cup powdered sugar

In small saucepan, combine butter, evaporated milk, brown sugar and salt. Cook and stir over low heat until sugar is dissolved.

Remove from heat and let cool. Stir in vanilla, then beat in powdered sugar until frosting consistency is reached.

Basic Cookie Dough Recipe on Page 7

Chocolate Covered Banana Bars

These yummy banana-flavored bars are moist and easy to make! Just add four ingredients to the Basic Cookie Dough to create. Frosting is almost automatic!

    1 recipe Basic Cookie Dough
    $1/3$ cup packed brown sugar
    1 cup mashed ripe bananas (about 2 large)
    $1/2$ cup sour cream
    2 cups milk chocolate or semi-sweet chocolate chips,
        divided

Preheat oven to 350°. In large bowl, combine Basic Cookie Dough with brown sugar, bananas and sour cream. Beat on medium high speed until mixture is smooth. Stir in 1 cup chocolate chips.

Spread batter in greased and floured 9 x 13-inch baking pan. Bake for 25 to 30 minutes or until cake tester comes out clean.

Immediately upon removing from oven, sprinkle remaining cup of chocolate chips evenly over surface and let them sit for 5 minutes. Spread softened chips over surface to frost. When cool, cut into bars and serve.

Notes

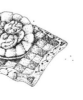

Notes

PART II

the

COOKIE CUTTER

COOKBOOK

When you were growing up did you ever eat a Christmas tree, a heart or star? Did you eat the head or arm off the gingerbread man first?

When we think about the answers to these questions, we travel back to another time and place where things were simple and tiny, little shiny red sprinkles made us smile from ear to ear and we were happy.

This Cookie Cutter cookbook is full of memories just like those in your mind and you can create new memories for your kids and the special people in your lives just by spending a few minutes to make very special cookies.

STARS, HEARTS, SHAMROCKS, BUNNIES, GINGERBREAD MEN AND CHRISTMAS TREES come alive with multi-colored candy sprinkles, red and green sugars, spray icings, red hots, yellow marshmallows, ground nuts, gum drops and who knows what else we can dream up to decorate these very special cookies.

Everything you need to make memories for a lifetime is here just for you.

CONTENTS
PART II

HOW TO DECORATE YOUR COOKIES

There are lots of ways to decorate the star, heart, bell, Christmas tree, bunny and gingerbread men. Just let your imagination be your guide and you and your children will have a great time.

Listed below are some of the possibilities for decorations on your cookies:

Colored decorating sugars
Colored sprinkles
Rainbow sprinkles
Colored nonpareils
Decorating stars
Edible cake decorations
Cake decorating letters
Writing icing
Decorating icings
Decorating sprays
Cinnamon candies
M & M's
Candles
Colored miniature marshmallows
Chocolate chips
White chocolate chips
Peanut butter and chocolate chips

Peanut butter chips
Butterscotch chips
Mini morsels
Raisins
Sweetened dried cranberries
Sliced almonds
Slivered almonds
Chopped nuts
Peanuts
Pecans
Walnuts
Assorted nuts
Sunflower seeds
Pumpkin seeds
Assorted dried fruits
Assorted fresh fruits

FROSTINGS, ICINGS AND SPRAYS

If you want any kind of frosting or icing on your cookies, the recipes below offer quick and easy ways to decorate with more than sprinkles and colored sugars. If you have no spare time, don't forget about the cans of frostings and icings in the grocery store near the cake mixes.

There are also handy squirt cans with icing, so you can write words or make your own designs. And if the squirt cans do not give you the look you want, find the fancy sprays that give a "big", thicker look. Kids cannot resist getting in on the act, and they will love to decorate their own cookies.

Use cookie cutters and cookie decorating for a rainy day or any day when you want to make memories with and for special people. It is just plain fun, any time for any person.

Here are some helpful frosting and icing recipes:

COLORED SNOW

1 cup powdered sugar
¼ teaspoon almond flavoring
Milk
Food coloring

Mix the powdered sugar and almond flavoring and slowly pour in milk a little at a time.

Stir and add a little milk until the mixture reaches a consistency that is easy to spread.

Add food coloring of your choice or leave it as white as snow.

COOKIE CUTTER TIP:
When you make frostings and icings, divide them into different bowls so you can make a different color in each bowl.

CREAMY, DREAMY ICING

1 cup (2 sticks) butter, softened
1 (1 pound) box powdered sugar
½ teaspoon vanilla or almond flavoring
⅛ teaspoon salt
Food colorings

Beat butter and powdered sugar together until very creamy.

Add Vanilla or almond flavoring and sale, blend together well.

If you want several different colors, divide the icing into different bowls so you can pour in the colors you want. Stir until the color is completely blended, and let yourself go.

COOKIE CUTTER TIP:

Vanilla is a great flavor to substitute, but regular vanilla leaves a tan tint to the icing. There is a clear vanilla, but it is hard to find. If you go to Mexico or have a friend going to Mexico, it is readily available and wonderful.

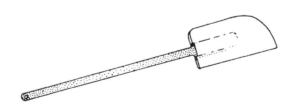

WHITE CLOUDS

1 (1 pound) box powdered sugar

¼ cup whipping cream, divided

½ teaspoon almond or clear vanilla

Dash salt

Pour powdered sugar in large bowl and gradually add about ⅛ cup or 2 tablespoons whipping cream and beat until smooth.

Add 1 tablespoon whipping cream and beat until creamy. If consistency is too thick to spread easily, add another tablespoon whipping cream.

COOKIE ICING

1 cup powdered sugar

2 teaspoons milk

2 teaspoons light corn syrup

coloring of your choice (paste works best)

Mix powdered sugar and milk.

Add corn syrup and mix well.

Stir in coloring and spread over cookies.

Sprinkle with your favorite sprinkles.

Lay on wax paper until set.

PART II

COOKIE CUTTER RECIPES

GINGERBREAD BOYS

½ cup molasses

2 cups sugar

2 eggs

1½ cups (3 sticks) butter, melted

4 cups flour

4 teaspoons baking soda

2 teaspoons cinnamon

1 teaspoon ground cloves

1 teaspoon ground ginger

Sugar

Preheat oven to 350°.

Add molasses, sugar and eggs to butter. Beat well. Combine flour, baking soda, cinnamon, cloves and ginger and stir into molasses-sugar mixture.

Cover bowl with plastic wrap and refrigerate for 3 to 4 hours.

Lay dough on waxed paper lightly sprinkled with flour. Roll out cookie dough to about ¼-inch thickness.

Dip edges of cookie cutter into flour or sugar so dough will not stick. Cut gingerbread boy shapes in dough as close as possible.

Lay each shape on baking pan about 1 inch apart.

Put all leftover dough to one side and make another large ball when there is enough dough. Roll-out and cut more shapes.

Sprinkle with sugar and decorate to make a face, buttons, belt and shoes with candy sprinkles.

Bake for about 8 to 10 minutes or until gingerbread men are brown.

GINGERBREAD ARMY

5 cups flour

1½ teaspoons baking soda

1 teaspoon ground ginger

½ teaspoon cinnamon

½ teaspoon ground cloves

½ teaspoon salt

1 cup (2 sticks) butter

1 cup sugar

1 egg

1 cup molasses

2 tablespoons vinegar

In large bowl combine flour, baking soda, ginger, cinnamon, cloves and salt and set aside.

In another large bowl, beat butter and sugar until creamy.

Stir in egg, molasses and vinegar until well mixed.

Slowly pour in flour and other dry ingredients and beat well. Cover with plastic wrap and refrigerate for 3 to 4 hours.

Lay dough on wax paper lightly sprinkled with flour. Roll out cookie dough to about ¼-inch thickness.

Dip edges of gingerbread man cookie cutter into flour or sugar so dough won't stick. Cut gingerbread man shapes in dough as close together as possible.

Lay each gingerbread man on baking pan about 1-inch apart and bake at 350° for 8 to 10 minutes or just until slightly brown.

Serve the gingerbread men just as they are or decorate them with red hots, colored sugars and candy sprinkles and have lots of fun. Make each one different.

BASIC COOKIE CUTTER COOKIES

¾ **cup sugar**

½ **cups (1 stick) butter, softened**

1 teaspoon vanilla or almond

2 cups flour

1 teaspoon baking soda

½ **teaspoon salt**

Mix together sugar, butter and vanilla to creamy consistency.

In separate bowl, mix flour, baking soda and salt. Slowly pour into sugar-butter mixture and mix well.

On lightly floured wax paper, roll out dough to ¼-inch thickness.

Dip edges of cookie cutters in sugar and cut out favorite shapes. Decorate with candy sprinkles and colored sugars.

Place on baking pan and bake at 350° for 10 to 12 minutes until lightly brown.

COOKIE CUTTER TIP:

For most cookie cutter recipes, it takes ¼ cup butter for every 1 cup flour to make dough easy to roll out without crumbling and being too dry.

Also, it works best when you refrigerate the dough and the baking pan, so the dough will not begin to melt and spread on the baking sheet.

ORNAMENT COOKIES

1 cup sugar

½ cup (1 stick) butter

1 egg

1½ teaspoon vanilla

2 cups flour

1 teaspoon baking powder

½ teaspoon salt

Colored sugars

Decorating sprinkles

Beat sugar and butter together until creamy. Stir in egg and vanilla.

In separate bowl mix flour, baking powder and salt. Stir into sugar mixture a little at a time. Cover and refrigerate 3 to 4 hours.

Divide dough into 2 batches and remove one from the refrigerator. On lightly floured wax paper, roll out dough to ¼-inch thickness.

Dip edges of cookie cutters into sugar or flour and cut out favorite shapes. Place on 9 x 13-inch baking pan.

With sharp knife or straw, make a hole at top of ornament for ribbon or string to hang on tree. Decorate with sprinkles and colored sugars before baking or frost with colored cake decorating icings or sprays after baking.

Bake at 350° for 10 to 12 minutes or until lightly brown.

CHOCOLATE TREES

Wouldn't it be nice if there were chocolate trees that grew chocolate leaves?

1 cup sugar

½ cup (1 stick) butter

1 egg

1 ½ teaspoon vanilla

2 cups flour

¼ cup cocoa

1 teaspoon baking powder

½ teaspoon salt

Colored sugars

Decorating sprinkles

Beat sugar and butter together until creamy. Stir in egg and vanilla.

In separate bowl mix flour, cocoa, baking powder and salt. Stir into sugar mixture a little at a time. Cover and refrigerate 3 to 4 hours.

Divide dough into 2 batches and remove one from the refrigerator. On lightly floured wax paper, roll out dough to ¼-inch thickness.

Dip edges of cookie cutters into sugar or flour and cut out tree shapes. Place on 9 x 13-inch baking pan.

Decorate with sprinkles and colored sugars before baking or frost with colored cake decorating icings or sprays after baking.

Bake at 350° for 10 to 12 minutes or until lightly brown.

BAYLOR COOKIES

This is an old family recipe dating back to 1944. Shortening is not used much any more, but it works well in this recipe.

1 cup shortening

¼ cup firmly packed brown sugar

1 cup sugar

1 egg

1½ teaspoons vanilla

⅓ teaspoon salt

2 cups flour

2 teaspoons baking powder

1 cup chopped nuts

Mix together shortening, sugars, egg and vanilla until creamy.

Add salt, flour and baking powder and mix thoroughly. Stir in nuts.

Batter will be stiff. Refrigerate several hours.

Divide batter into 2 batches and roll on lightly floured wax paper to about ¼-inch thickness.

Dip edges of cookie cutter in sugar or flour and cut out favorite shapes.

Bake at 350° for about 8 to 10 minutes or until lightly browned.

SWEET CRUSTS

This is an old-fashioned, basic pie crust recipe. When there were left-over pieces of dough after Mother finished putting the crust into the pie pan, she sprinkled sugar and cinnamon over them and baked them like cookies. It always seemed like we were getting something extra special. This recipe makes two pie crusts. Just make one pie and use the other crust to give the kids those extra special pieces.

2 cups flour

2 teaspoons sugar

1 teaspoon ground cinnamon, optional

¼ cup ground pecans, optional

¼ teaspoon salt

1 cup shortening, chilled

½ cup (8 tablespoons) ice water, divided

Mix together flour, sugar, cinnamon, pecans and salt.

Blend in shortening a little at a time, and slowly pour in ice water a little at a time to get smooth, but stiff consistency. Mix with hands, back of big spoon or pastry knife until it rolls into a ball.

Cover and refrigerate for several hours.

Divide dough into 2 batches and roll out each on lightly floured wax paper to about ⅛-inch thickness.

Dip edges of cookie cutters in sugar or powdered sugar and cut out favorite shapes. Place on baking pan and decorate with cake decorating sprinkles, morsels and sticks.

Bake at 375° for 8 to 10 minutes or until lightly brown.

CRUSTY CUT-OUTS

This is another old-fashioned, basic pie crust recipe. It's not as sweet as Sweet Crusts on page 16, but it is still a sure winner. Make one pie and use the other pie crust for special little pieces for the kids.

2 cups flour

½ teaspoon salt

1 teaspoon allspice, optional

¼ cup ground nuts, optional

¾ cup shortening, chilled

⅓ cup (5-6 tablespoons) ice water, divided

Mix together flour, salt, allspice and pecans.

Blend in shortening a little at a time and slowly pour in ice water a little at a time to get smooth, but stiff consistency until it rolls into a ball.

Cover and refrigerate for several hours.

Divide dough into two batches and roll out each batch to about ⅛-inch thickness on lightly floured wax paper.

Dip edges of cookie cutters in sugar or powdered sugar and cut out favorite shapes. Place on baking pan and decorate with cake decorating sprinkles, morsels and sticks.

Bake at 375° for 8 to 10 minutes or until lightly brown.

COOKIE CUTTER TIP:

Add ice water a little at a time to get the right consistency for pie crust. Too little water makes the crust crumble and hard to roll out. Too much water hurts the flaky texture and makes it tough.

SWEETHEART COOKIES
SUPER EASY!

1 (20 ounce) package refrigerated sugar cookie dough

1 (16 ounce) can white frosting

Red Food Coloring

Powdered sugar

Decorating stars, hearts and sprinkles

On light floured waxed paper, roll out dough to ¼-inch thickness.

Dip edges of heart-shaped cookie cutter in sugar and cut out as many hearts as possible. Place on baking pan.

With sharp knife, cut out smaller heart from inside half the hearts and separate from the outside. Put smaller heart on top of half the hearts that have not had smaller hearts removed.

Bake at 350° for about 8 to 10 minutes. Use food coloring to tint frosting and spread on cookies. Decorate with stars, tiny hearts and sprinkles.

CHOCOLATE CHI
COOKIE STICKS

½ cup sugar

½ cup packed brown sugar

½ cup oil

1 teaspoon vanilla

1 egg

1 ½ cups flour

½ teaspoon baking soda

¼ teaspoon salt

1 cup semi-sweet chocolate chips

½ cup chopped pecans

Preheat oven at 350°.

In mixing bowl, mix both sugars, oil, vanilla and egg until smooth.

In a separate bowl combine flour, baking soda and salt and gradually add to sugar mixture.

Divide dough into quarters. Shape each quarter into a 15 x 3-inch strip and place on lightly greased baking sheet about 3 inches apart.

Sprinkle each strip with ¼ the chocolate chips and pecans and press lightly.

Bake for 8-10 minutes.

Cool slightly and cut each strip crosswise into 1-inch slices.

SPRINGERLE COOKIES

Springerle Cookies are a traditional German Christmas cookie in which a carved rolling pin is used to make a design similar to a jigsaw puzzle on the rolled out dough. Cookies are cut apart long the lines made by the carved rolling pin. We use the recipe for cookie cutter shapes.

4 eggs

1 (16 ounce) box powdered sugar

1 teaspoon butter, softened

4 cups flour, divided

½ teaspoon baking powder

¼ teaspoon salt

½ teaspoon anise oil or

2 teaspoons small anise seed, optional

1½ teaspoons grated lemon rind

Beat eggs until light and fluffy. Add sugar gradually, beating on high speed until soft peaks form, about 15 minutes. Beat in butter.

Blend in 2 cups flour, baking powder and salt until thoroughly mixed. Stir in 1½ cups flour, anise oil and lemon rind.

Sprinkle remaining 1/2 cup flour on wax paper. Divide dough into 2 batches. Roll each piece to about ½-inch thickness. Let stand 1 minute.

Dip edges of cookie cutters in sugar or flour and cut out shapes.

Place on greased baking pan, cover with towel and refrigerate overnight.

Decorate with favorite sprinkles, morsels or sticks before baking or decorator frostings, icings or sprays after baking.

Bake at 300° for 15 to 20 minutes or until light brown and dry.

COOKIES DRESSED FOR CHRISTMAS

1 cup (2 sticks) butter, softened
1 cup sugar
1 egg, beaten
1 teaspoon vanilla
2¾ cups flour
1 teaspoon baking powder
¼ teaspoon salt
1 (16 ounce) jar maraschino cherries,
well drained, finely chopped
1 cup slivered almonds
⅓ cup red decorator sugar crystals

In mixing bowl, beat butter and sugar until creamy and gradually add egg and vanilla, mixing well.

Add flour, baking powder and salt to the creamy mixture and beat well.

Drain chopped cherries in several paper towels to remove all moisture.

Stir cherries and almonds into the dough and cover and chill for several hours.

Shape dough into 2 (8½-inch) rolls.

Roll in decorator sugar crystals.

Wrap rolls in wax paper and chill until firm or freeze.

Use a sharp knife to slice rolls into ¼-inch slices. Place on greased baking sheet.

Bake at 350° for 8-10 minutes. Cool before storing.

GINGER CRINKLES

1 cup (2 sticks) margarine, softened

⅓ cup shortening

2 cups sugar

2 eggs

½ cup molasses

3 teaspoons baking soda

½ teaspoon salt

2 teaspoons cinnamon

½ teaspoon cloves

2 teaspoons ginger

4½ cups flour

Sugar

Powdered sugar

Preheat oven at 350°.

In a mixing bowl, thoroughly cream together margarine, shortening, sugar, eggs and molasses and beat well.

Stir in the baking soda, salt, cinnamon, cloves and ginger.

Add flour and mix well.

Shape cookies into 1-inch balls and chill. Roll in sugar.

Bake for about 12 minutes.

Sprinkle powdered sugar over top of warm cookies with shaker or sift through a strainer.

To make gingerbread men chill dough, then roll out on floured board and cut with cookie cutter in shape of gingerbread man. Decorate or sprinkle with granulated sugar.

DATE-FILLED COOKIES

1 cup packed brown sugar

½ cup milk

½ teaspoon baking powder

1 cup shortening

1 teaspoon baking soda

2 cups quick oatmeal

2½ cups flour

Mix together and chill dough. Roll very thin and bake in a 375° oven, watch carefully.

Cool.

FILLING

1 (16 ounce) package dates, cut very fine

1 cup sugar

1 cup water

Mix until well blended.

Filling may be refrigerated. Before serving spread between two cookies to make a cookie sandwich.

CANDY BAR COOKIES

¾ cup butter

¾ cup sifted powdered sugar

1 teaspoon vanilla

¼ teaspoon salt

2 cups flour

2 tablespoons evaporated milk

Cream butter and sugar, add vanilla, milk and salt. Add flour.

Roll out dough half at a time ⅛ inch thick. Cut into rounds or squares. Bake at 325° until golden brown.

Cool and spread filling between cookies.

CARAMEL FILLING

½ lb. light caramels

¼ cup evaporated milk

¼ cup butter

1 cup sifted powdered sugar

1 cup chopped pecans (optional)

Combine caramels and milk in top of double broiler. Heat until caramels melt. Stir occasionally.

Remove from heat. Keep top of double broiler over hot water.

Add butter and powdered sugar, mix well.

Stir in nuts.

ROCKY'S STAR BISCUITS

Don't leave out your dog when you are making cookies. Make these great doggie treats with cookie cutter shapes he loves.

1 ½ cups white or whole wheat flour

½ cup bran cereal

½ cup rolled oats

1 egg

½ cup lowfat milk

¼ cup oil

¼ cup chicken broth

Stir together flour, cereal and oats in bowl.

In separate bowl, scramble egg with fork and stir in milk, oil and chicken broth.

Pour liquid mixture into flour-cereal mixture and mix well.

On waxed paper lightly sprinkled with flour, roll out dough on to about ¼-inch thickness.

Cut treats into stars or your dog's favorite shapes with cookie cutters.

Place on sprayed baking pan about 1 inch apart.

Bake at 350° for 10 to 12 minutes. Remove from oven and let stars harden overnight or leave in oven overnight to make extra hard treats.

NOTES

Gifts For The Cookie Jar

Cookie Recipes
for Ingredients in a Jar

Lia Roessner Wilson

Contents – PART III

YOUR GIFT JARS
CAN BE SPECTACULAR

Dressing up your gift jar is limited only by your imagination, so have fun! This is an excellent craft project for older children and even the little ones can help paint, glue and decorate. Gather your supplies and enjoy some time together. With fabric, ribbon and colored pens you can quickly and inexpensively personalize your gift jars for that special person or occasion.

TOP IT!

Ideas:

- Paint lid and decorate with buttons, charms, shells, beads or old costume jewelry.
- Lace Doilies: Place $6^1/_2$ –7-inch doily over a painted lid or a solid color circle of fabric. You may be able to lace ribbon through and tie in a bow.
- Brown craft paper (brown paper bag) cut in a $6^1/_2$ –7-inch circle. This looks very country if tied with natural or red raffia.
- Fabric cut in $6^1/_2$-7-inch circle or 2, $6^1/_2$ –7-inch squares of coordinating fabric. Place the first square on top of the second so that the points are centered on the straight edge. The catty-corner placement produces a cute handkerchief hem.

Pointers:

- Cutting with pinking shears or fancy edge scissors will finish the edge nicely. Use a pencil to trace a $6^1/_2$ –7-inch circle or square on the wrong side of your fabric. A plate or lid works well for a quick pattern. If you are making more than one topper, you will want to layer as many fabrics as your scissors will comfortably cut. Pin your layers together and cut.
- Edges of lace, fringe or beading may be applied by either sewing or gluing.
- Center the topper on the jar lid and secure with a rubber band.

TIE IT!

Ideas:
- ✂ Ribbon   ✂ Wired Ribbon   ✂ Jute   ✂ Cording   ✂ Raffia
- ✂ Narrow Ribbon – use several strands of the same or complementary colors.
- ✂ Weave a ribbon through straight or ruffled lace and tie in a bow. If using straight lace cut it twice the length to go around the lid.
- ✂ Decorative Wire Garland (stars, snowflakes, hearts etc.) Wrap the wire around the lid several times and twist to secure. If you leave a tail of 6 inches on both sides you can curl them by coiling the wire around a pencil.

Pointers:
- Slant- cut the ends of the streamers.
- Fold ribbon edges together lengthwise and cut a slant from the edge up toward the fold. This technique gives you a two- pointed tail on the streamer.
- Knot each ribbon streamer a couple of times at different intervals. This is an attractive look when using several strands of narrow ribbons.
- Knot only the ends of each streamer. It's a great look for jute or cording.
- Tie small jingle bells, buttons or charms to each streamer.
- Loop a couple of small tassels around cording.

TAG IT!

Each recipe has 6 tags, which include the baking instructions.
- Photocopy or simply cut apart and attach to the jar.
- Use colored pens to add a little zip.
- There is plenty of room for a greeting or use one of the friendship quotes from the book. In a hurry? Use a tag with a pre-printed greeting.

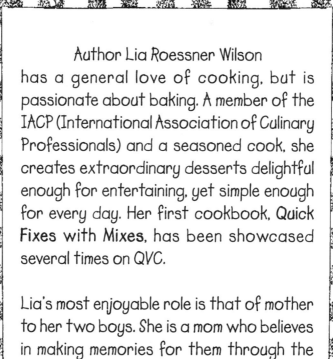

Author Lia Roessner Wilson has a general love of cooking, but is passionate about baking. A member of the IACP (International Association of Culinary Professionals) and a seasoned cook, she creates extraordinary desserts delightful enough for entertaining, yet simple enough for every day. Her first cookbook, **Quick Fixes** with **Mixes**, has been showcased several times on QVC.

Lia's most enjoyable role is that of mother to her two boys. She is a mom who believes in making memories for them through the wonderful aromas and treats from her kitchen – the kind of memories that will be remembered for a lifetime.

Spicy Oatmeal-Raisin Cookies

Spicy Oatmeal-Raisin Cookies

These delicious, soft, oatmeal-raisin cookies have a light spicy flavor. As they bake, their aroma fills the kitchen with a sweet, homey fragrance.

Ingredients for jar:

$^3/_4$ cup packed light brown sugar
$^1/_3$ cup sugar
$^3/_4$ teaspoon allspice
$^3/_4$ teaspoon baking powder
$^1/_8$ teaspoon baking soda
1 cup flour
1 cup quick-cooking oats
$^3/_4$ cup raisins
$^1/_2$ cup chopped walnuts

Instructions for jar:

1. In a 1-quart jar, pack brown sugar in bottom and make as level as possible. Pour sugar over and level.
2. In small bowl, combine allspice, baking powder, baking soda and flour. Mix well. Gently spoon flour mixture over sugar. Level carefully, then tamp down.
3. Pour oats over flour and level. Sprinkle raisins on top and press down. Sprinkle nuts over raisins. Place lid on jar.

Spicy Oatmeal-Raisin Cookies

Instructions for baking:

1 egg
$^1/_2$ cup (1 stick) butter, softened

1. Preheat oven to 375°. Pour contents of jar into large mixing bowl. Add egg and softened margarine or butter.

2. Beat on low speed or mix by hand until mixture is thoroughly blended.

3. Drop by rounded teaspoonfuls onto ungreased cookie sheet. Bake for 10 to 12 minutes.

4. Remove from oven and let cookies cool on cookie sheet for 1 minute. Transfer to cooling rack. (Makes 2 to $2^1/_2$ dozen.)

Icing (optional):

1 cup powdered sugar, divided
1-2 tablespoons milk
$^1/_4$ teaspoon vanilla

1. In small bowl, combine powdered sugar with 1 tablespoon milk and vanilla. Stir until smooth, adding additional milk as necessary until drizzling consistency is reached. Drizzle over cookies and let set.

Spicy Oatmeal-Raisin Cookies

1 egg
$^1/_2$ cup (1 stick) butter, softened

1. Preheat oven to 375°. Pour mixture in jar into large mixing bowl. Add egg and softened margarine or butter.
2. Beat on low speed or mix by hand until mixture is thoroughly blended.
3. Drop by rounded teaspoonfuls onto ungreased cookie sheet. Bake for 10 to 12 minutes.
4. Remove from oven and let cookies cool on cookie sheet for 1 minute. Transfer to cooling rack. (Makes 2 to 2$^1/_2$ dozen.)

Icing (optional):
1 cup powdered sugar, divided
1-2 tablespoons milk
$^1/_4$ teaspoon vanilla

1. In small bowl, combine powdered sugar with 1 tablespoon milk and vanilla. Stir until smooth, adding additional milk as necessary until drizzling consistency is reached. Drizzle over cookies and let set.

www.cookbookresources.com

Spicy Oatmeal-Raisin Cookies

1 egg
$^1/_2$ cup (1 stick) butter, softened

1. Preheat oven to 375°. Pour mixture in jar into large mixing bowl. Add egg and softened margarine or butter.
2. Beat on low speed or mix by hand until mixture is thoroughly blended.
3. Drop by rounded teaspoonfuls onto ungreased cookie sheet. Bake for 10 to 12 minutes.
4. Remove from oven and let cookies cool on cookie sheet for 1 minute. Transfer to cooling rack. (Makes 2 to 2$^1/_2$ dozen.)

Icing (optional):
1 cup powdered sugar, divided
1-2 tablespoons milk
$^1/_4$ teaspoon vanilla

1. In small bowl, combine powdered sugar with 1 tablespoon milk and vanilla. Stir until smooth, adding additional milk as necessary until drizzling consistency is reached. Drizzle over cookies and let set.

www.cookbookresources.com

Spicy Oatmeal-Raisin Cookies

1 egg
$^1/_2$ cup (1 stick) butter, softened

1. Preheat oven to 375°. Pour mixture in jar into large mixing bowl. Add egg and softened margarine or butter.
2. Beat on low speed or mix by hand until mixture is thoroughly blended.
3. Drop by rounded teaspoonfuls onto ungreased cookie sheet. Bake for 10 to 12 minutes.
4. Remove from oven and let cookies cool on cookie sheet for 1 minute. Transfer to cooling rack. (Makes 2 to 2$^1/_2$ dozen.)

Icing (optional):
1 cup powdered sugar, divided
1-2 tablespoons milk
$^1/_4$ teaspoon vanilla

1. In small bowl, combine powdered sugar with 1 tablespoon milk and vanilla. Stir until smooth, adding additional milk as necessary until drizzling consistency is reached. Drizzle over cookies and let set.

www.cookbookresources.com

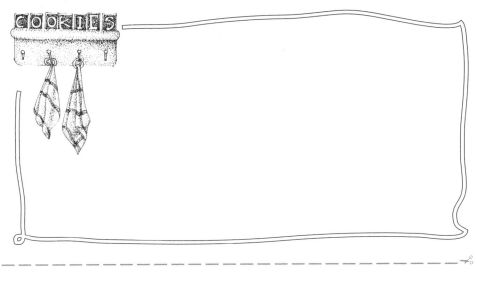

You're a Doll

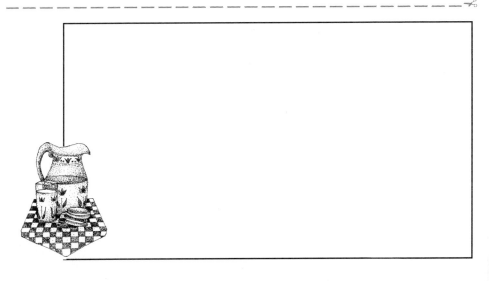

Spicy Oatmeal-Raisin Cookies

1 egg
1/2 cup (1 stick) butter, softened

1. Preheat oven to 375°. Pour mixture in jar into large mixing bowl. Add egg and softened margarine or butter.
2. Beat on low speed or mix by hand until mixture is thoroughly blended.
3. Drop by rounded teaspoonfuls onto ungreased cookie sheet. Bake for 10 to 12 minutes.
4. Remove from oven and let cookies cool on cookie sheet for 1 minute. Transfer to cooling rack. (Makes 2 to 2 1/2 dozen.)

Icing (optional):

1 cup powdered sugar, divided
1-2 tablespoons milk
1/4 teaspoon vanilla

1. In small bowl, combine powdered sugar with 1 tablespoon milk and vanilla. Stir until smooth, adding additional milk as necessary until drizzling consistency is reached. Drizzle over cookies and let set.

www.cookbookresources.com

Spicy Oatmeal-Raisin Cookies

1 egg
1/2 cup (1 stick) butter, softened

1. Preheat oven to 375°. Pour mixture in jar into large mixing bowl. Add egg and softened margarine or butter.
2. Beat on low speed or mix by hand until mixture is thoroughly blended.
3. Drop by rounded teaspoonfuls onto ungreased cookie sheet. Bake for 10 to 12 minutes.
4. Remove from oven and let cookies cool on cookie sheet for 1 minute. Transfer to cooling rack. (Makes 2 to 2 1/2 dozen.)

Icing (optional):

1 cup powdered sugar, divided
1-2 tablespoons milk
1/4 teaspoon vanilla

1. In small bowl, combine powdered sugar with 1 tablespoon milk and vanilla. Stir until smooth, adding additional milk as necessary until drizzling consistency is reached. Drizzle over cookies and let set.

www.cookbookresources.com

Spicy Oatmeal-Raisin Cookies

1 egg
1/2 cup (1 stick) butter, softened

1. Preheat oven to 375°. Pour mixture in jar into large mixing bowl. Add egg and softened margarine or butter.
2. Beat on low speed or mix by hand until mixture is thoroughly blended.
3. Drop by rounded teaspoonfuls onto ungreased cookie sheet. Bake for 10 to 12 minutes.
4. Remove from oven and let cookies cool on cookie sheet for 1 minute. Transfer to cooling rack. (Makes 2 to 2 1/2 dozen.)

Icing (optional):

1 cup powdered sugar, divided
1-2 tablespoons milk
1/4 teaspoon vanilla

1. In small bowl, combine powdered sugar with 1 tablespoon milk and vanilla. Stir until smooth, adding additional milk as necessary until drizzling consistency is reached. Drizzle over cookies and let set.

www.cookbookresources.com

Happy Birthday

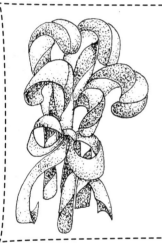

Happy Holidays

Merry Christmas!

Chunky Chocolate Cookies

Chunky Chocolate Cookies

Truly this is the cookie for a chocoholic. These soft chocolate cookies are studded with dark chocolate and white chocolate chips.

Ingredients for jar:

$2/3$ cup packed dark brown sugar
$1/2$ cup sugar
$1^1/2$ cups flour
$1/3$ cup cocoa powder
$1/2$ teaspoon baking soda
Pinch salt
$3/4$ cup semi-sweet chocolate chips
$3/4$ cup white chocolate chips

Instructions for jar:

1. In a 1-quart jar, pack brown sugar in bottom and make as level as possible. Pour sugar over and level.
2. In small bowl, combine flour, cocoa powder, baking soda, and salt. Mix well. Gently spoon flour mixture over sugar. Level carefully, then tamp down.
3. Pour semi-sweet chocolate chips on top of flour, then sprinkle white chocolate chips over and level. Place lid on jar.

Chunky Chocolate Cookies

Instructions for baking:

1 egg
$^3/_4$ cup ($1^1/_2$ sticks) butter, softened

1. Preheat oven to 350°. Pour contents of jar into large mixing bowl. Add egg and softened butter or margarine.

2. Beat on low speed or by hand until mixture is thoroughly blended.

3. Drop by heaping teaspoonfuls onto ungreased cookie sheet. Bake for 13 to 15 minutes. Remove from oven and let cookies cool on cookie sheet for 1 minute. Transfer to cooling rack. (Makes about 3 dozen.)

"To know someone here or there with whom you can feel there is understanding in spite of distances or thoughts expressed ~ That can make life a garden."

Goethe

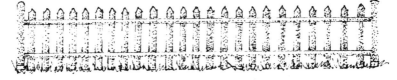

Chunky Chocolate Cookies

1 egg
$^3/_4$ cup (1$^1/_2$ sticks) butter, softened

1. Preheat oven to 350°. Pour contents of jar into large mixing bowl. Add egg and softened butter or margarine.
2. Beat on low speed or by hand until mixture is thoroughly blended.
3. Drop by heaping teaspoonfuls onto ungreased cookie sheet. Bake for 13 to 15 minutes. Remove from oven and let cookies cool on cookie sheet for 1 minute. Transfer to cooling rack. (Makes about 3 dozen.)

www.cookbookresources.com

Chunky Chocolate Cookies

1 egg
$^3/_4$ cup (1$^1/_2$ sticks) butter, softened

1. Preheat oven to 350°. Pour contents of jar into large mixing bowl. Add egg and softened butter or margarine.
2. Beat on low speed or by hand until mixture is thoroughly blended.
3. Drop by heaping teaspoonfuls onto ungreased cookie sheet. Bake for 13 to 15 minutes. Remove from oven and let cookies cool on cookie sheet for 1 minute. Transfer to cooling rack. (Makes about 3 dozen.)

www.cookbookresources.com

Chunky Chocolate Cookies

1 egg
$^3/_4$ cup (1$^1/_2$ sticks) butter, softened

1. Preheat oven to 350°. Pour contents of jar into large mixing bowl. Add egg and softened butter or margarine.
2. Beat on low speed or by hand until mixture is thoroughly blended.
3. Drop by heaping teaspoonfuls onto ungreased cookie sheet. Bake for 13 to 15 minutes. Remove from oven and let cookies cool on cookie sheet for 1 minute. Transfer to cooling rack. (Makes about 3 dozen.)

www.cookbookresources.com

Thinking of You

Chunky Chocolate Cookies

1 egg
$^3/_4$ cup (1$^1/_2$ sticks) butter, softened

1. Preheat oven to 350°. Pour contents of jar into large mixing bowl. Add egg and softened butter or margarine.
2. Beat on low speed or by hand until mixture is thoroughly blended.
3. Drop by heaping teaspoonfuls onto ungreased cookie sheet. Bake for 13 to 15 minutes. Remove from oven and let cookies cool on cookie sheet for 1 minute. Transfer to cooling rack. (Makes about 3 dozen.)

www.cookbookresources.com

Chunky Chocolate Cookies

1 egg
$^3/_4$ cup (1$^1/_2$ sticks) butter, softened

1. Preheat oven to 350°. Pour contents of jar into large mixing bowl. Add egg and softened butter or margarine.
2. Beat on low speed or by hand until mixture is thoroughly blended.
3. Drop by heaping teaspoonfuls onto ungreased cookie sheet. Bake for 13 to 15 minutes. Remove from oven and let cookies cool on cookie sheet for 1 minute. Transfer to cooling rack. (Makes about 3 dozen.)

www.cookbookresources.com

Chunky Chocolate Cookies

1 egg
$^3/_4$ cup (1$^1/_2$ sticks) butter, softened

1. Preheat oven to 350°. Pour contents of jar into large mixing bowl. Add egg and softened butter or margarine.
2. Beat on low speed or by hand until mixture is thoroughly blended.
3. Drop by heaping teaspoonfuls onto ungreased cookie sheet. Bake for 13 to 15 minutes. Remove from oven and let cookies cool on cookie sheet for 1 minute. Transfer to cooling rack. (Makes about 3 dozen.)

www.cookbookresources.com

Happy
Birthday

Happy Holidays

Merry Christmas

Hearty Trail Mix Cookies

Hearty Trail Mix Cookies

These hearty cookies are filled with natural goodness--oats, raisins, and coconut--as well as with a chocolate treat. They're not only delicious, but colorful too. The candies provide a rainbow of color throughout.

Ingredients for jar:
$1/2$ cup packed brown sugar
$1/4$ cup sugar
1 cup quick-cooking oats
1 cup flour
$1/2$ teaspoon baking powder
$1/8$ teaspoon baking soda
$1/2$ cup raisins
$1/2$ cup coconut
$1/2$ cup M&M candies

Instructions for jar:
1. In a 1-quart jar, pack brown sugar in bottom and make as level as possible. Pour sugar over and level.
2. Pour oats over sugar and level.
3. In small bowl, combine flour, baking powder and baking soda. Mix well. Gently spoon flour mixture over oats. Level carefully, then tamp down.
4. Sprinkle raisins over flour mixture, level and smooth the edges to make them even. Sprinkle raisins on top and press down. Sprinkle coconut over raisins and press down.
5. Sprinkle candies on top. Press down and place lid on jar.

Hearty Trail Mix Cookies
Instructions for baking:

1 egg
6 tablespoons butter, softened

1. Preheat oven to 375°. Empty contents of jar into large mixing bowl. Add 1 egg and 6 tablespoons softened butter or margarine.

2. Beat on low speed or by hand to blend, then drop by heaping teaspoonfuls onto ungreased cookie sheet. Bake for 10 to 12 minutes or until edges are lightly browned.

3. Remove from oven and let cookies cool on cookie sheet for 1 minute, then transfer to cooling rack. (Makes about 3 dozen.)

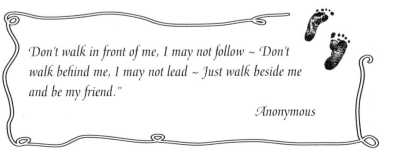

Don't walk in front of me, I may not follow ~ Don't walk behind me, I may not lead ~ Just walk beside me and be my friend."

Anonymous

Hearty Trail Mix Cookies

1 egg
6 tablespoons butter, softened

1. Preheat oven to 375°. Empty contents of jar into large mixing bowl. Add egg and softened butter or margarine.
2. Beat on low speed or by hand to blend, then drop by heaping teaspoonfuls onto ungreased cookie sheet. Bake for 10 to 12 minutes or until edges are lightly browned.
3. Remove from oven and let cookies cool on cookie sheet for 1 minute, then transfer to cooling rack. (Makes about 3 dozen.)

www.cookbookresources.com

Hearty Trail Mix Cookies

1 egg
6 tablespoons butter, softened

1. Preheat oven to 375°. Empty contents of jar into large mixing bowl. Add egg and softened butter or margarine.
2. Beat on low speed or by hand to blend, then drop by heaping teaspoonfuls onto ungreased cookie sheet. Bake for 10 to 12 minutes or until edges are lightly browned.
3. Remove from oven and let cookies cool on cookie sheet for 1 minute, then transfer to cooling rack. (Makes about 3 dozen.)

www.cookbookresources.com

Hearty Trail Mix Cookies

1 egg
6 tablespoons butter, softened

1. Preheat oven to 375°. Empty contents of jar into large mixing bowl. Add egg and softened butter or margarine.
2. Beat on low speed or by hand to blend, then drop by heaping teaspoonfuls onto ungreased cookie sheet. Bake for 10 to 12 minutes or until edges are lightly browned.
3. Remove from oven and let cookies cool on cookie sheet for 1 minute, then transfer to cooling rack. (Makes about 3 dozen.)

www.cookbookresources.com

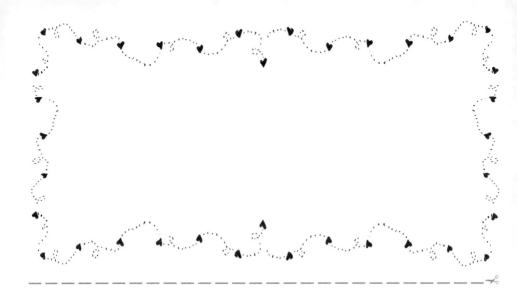

You're a Pal

Hearty Trail Mix Cookies

1 egg
6 tablespoons butter, softened

1. Preheat oven to 375°. Empty contents of jar into large mixing bowl. Add egg and softened butter or margarine.
2. Beat on low speed or by hand to blend, then drop by heaping teaspoonfuls onto ungreased cookie sheet. Bake for 10 to 12 minutes or until edges are lightly browned.
3. Remove from oven and let cookies cool on cookie sheet for 1 minute, then transfer to cooling rack. (Makes about 3 dozen.)

www.cookbookresources.com

Hearty Trail Mix Cookies

1 egg
6 tablespoons butter, softened

1. Preheat oven to 375°. Empty contents of jar into large mixing bowl. Add egg and softened butter or margarine.
2. Beat on low speed or by hand to blend, then drop by heaping teaspoonfuls onto ungreased cookie sheet. Bake for 10 to 12 minutes or until edges are lightly browned.
3. Remove from oven and let cookies cool on cookie sheet for 1 minute, then transfer to cooling rack. (Makes about 3 dozen.)

www.cookbookresources.com

Hearty Trail Mix Cookies

1 egg
6 tablespoons butter, softened

1. Preheat oven to 375°. Empty contents of jar into large mixing bowl. Add egg and softened butter or margarine.
2. Beat on low speed or by hand to blend, then drop by heaping teaspoonfuls onto ungreased cookie sheet. Bake for 10 to 12 minutes or until edges are lightly browned.
3. Remove from oven and let cookies cool on cookie sheet for 1 minute, then transfer to cooling rack. (Makes about 3 dozen.)

www.cookbookresources.com

Happy Birthday

Happy Holidays

Merry Christmas

Festive Cranberry-Orange Cookies

Festive Cranberry-Orange Cookies

Cranberry and orange flavors are great companions. This cookie lets the flavors shine through. The taste of the crunchy, lightly orange-flavored cookie is accented by sweet, red cranberries sprinkled throughout.

Ingredients for jar:

1 cup packed light brown sugar
$1/2$ cup sugar
$2^1/4$ cups flour
1 teaspoon baking soda
$1/4$ teaspoon salt
1 tablespoon dried, orange peel*
$3/4$ cup chopped dried, sweetened cranberries

Instructions for jar:

1. Place brown sugar in 1-quart jar and pack down.
2. Next, pour sugar on top and smooth over.
3. In medium bowl, combine flour, baking soda, salt and orange peel. Stir until well mixed. Pour half of mixture on top of sugar in jar and press down. Pour remaining half in jar, press down and smooth over top.
4. Pour cranberries over flour and press down. Place lid on top of jar.

* Dried, ground orange peel can be found in the spice section of the grocery store.

Festive Cranberry-Orange Cookies
Instructions for baking:

1 cup (2 sticks) butter, softened
2 eggs

1. Preheat oven to 350°. Empty contents of jar in large bowl. Add softened butter or margarine and eggs.

2. Beat until thoroughly mixed.

3. Drop by rounded teaspoonfuls onto ungreased cookie sheet and bake for 10 to 12 minutes until lightly browned around edges.

4. Remove from oven and let cookies cool on cookie sheet for 1 minute, then transfer to cooling rack. (Makes 3 to $3^{1}/_{2}$ dozen.)

Sometimes our light goes out but is blown into flame by another human being. Each of us owes deepest thanks to those who have rekindled this light."
                                                    Albert Schweitzer

Festive Cranberry-Orange Cookies

1 cup (2 sticks) butter, softened
2 eggs

1. Preheat oven to 350°. Empty contents of jar in large bowl. Add softened butter or margarine and eggs.
2. Beat until thoroughly mixed.
3. Drop by rounded teaspoonfuls onto ungreased cookie sheet and bake for 10 to 12 minutes until lightly browned around edges.
4. Remove from oven and let cookies cool on cookie sheet for 1 minute, then transfer to cooling rack. (Makes 3 to $3^1/_2$ dozen.)

www.cookbookresources.com

Festive Cranberry-Orange Cookies

1 cup (2 sticks) butter, softened
2 eggs

1. Preheat oven to 350°. Empty contents of jar in large bowl. Add softened butter or margarine and eggs.
2. Beat until thoroughly mixed.
3. Drop by rounded teaspoonfuls onto ungreased cookie sheet and bake for 10 to 12 minutes until lightly browned around edges.
4. Remove from oven and let cookies cool on cookie sheet for 1 minute, then transfer to cooling rack. (Makes 3 to $3^1/_2$ dozen.)

www.cookbookresources.com

Festive Cranberry-Orange Cookies

1 cup (2 sticks) butter, softened
2 eggs

1. Preheat oven to 350°. Empty contents of jar in large bowl. Add softened butter or margarine and eggs.
2. Beat until thoroughly mixed.
3. Drop by rounded teaspoonfuls onto ungreased cookie sheet and bake for 10 to 12 minutes until lightly browned around edges.
4. Remove from oven and let cookies cool on cookie sheet for 1 minute, then transfer to cooling rack. (Makes 3 to $3^1/_2$ dozen.)

www.cookbookresources.com

Best Wishes

Festive Cranberry-Orange Cookies

1 cup (2 sticks) butter, softened
2 eggs

1. Preheat oven to 350°. Empty contents of jar in large bowl. Add softened butter or margarine and eggs.
2. Beat until thoroughly mixed.
3. Drop by rounded teaspoonfuls onto ungreased cookie sheet and bake for 10 to 12 minutes until lightly browned around edges.
4. Remove from oven and let cookies cool on cookie sheet for 1 minute, then transfer to cooling rack. (Makes 3 to 3^1/$_2$ dozen.)

www.cookbookresources.com

Festive Cranberry-Orange Cookies

1 cup (2 sticks) butter, softened
2 eggs

1. Preheat oven to 350°. Empty contents of jar in large bowl. Add softened butter or margarine and eggs.
2. Beat until thoroughly mixed.
3. Drop by rounded teaspoonfuls onto ungreased cookie sheet and bake for 10 to 12 minutes until lightly browned around edges.
4. Remove from oven and let cookies cool on cookie sheet for 1 minute, then transfer to cooling rack. (Makes 3 to 3^1/$_2$ dozen.)

www.cookbookresources.com

Festive Cranberry-Orange Cookies

1 cup (2 sticks) butter, softened
2 eggs

1. Preheat oven to 350°. Empty contents of jar in large bowl. Add softened butter or margarine and eggs.
2. Beat until thoroughly mixed.
3. Drop by rounded teaspoonfuls onto ungreased cookie sheet and bake for 10 to 12 minutes until lightly browned around edges.
4. Remove from oven and let cookies cool on cookie sheet for 1 minute, then transfer to cooling rack. (Makes 3 to 3^1/$_2$ dozen.)

www.cookbookresources.com

Happy Birthday

Happy Holidays

Merry Christmas

Wholesome Peanut Butter Cookies

Wholesome Peanut Butter Cookies

These soft peanut butter cookies are a hit. The oats add a wonderful texture.

Ingredients for jar:
$1/2$ cup packed brown sugar
1 cup sugar
2 cups quick-cooking oats
1 cup plus 2 tablespoons flour
1 teaspoon baking powder
$1/2$ teaspoon baking soda
$1/4$ teaspoon salt

Instructions for jar:
1. Place brown sugar in 1-quart jar and press down evenly.
2. Pour sugar over brown sugar and smooth top.
3. Pour oats over sugar.
4. In small bowl, mix flour, baking powder, baking soda and salt. Pour half of mixture on oats and press down firmly. Add remaining flour mixture a little at a time, pressing down after each addition. (It will be a tight squeeze.)
5. Place lid on jar.

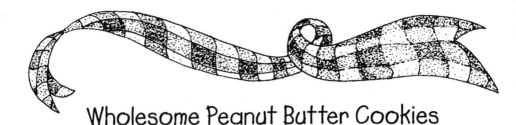

Wholesome Peanut Butter Cookies
Instructions for baking:

2 eggs
$1/2$ cup crunchy or creamy peanut butter
$3/4$ cup ($1^1/2$ sticks) butter, softened
$1^1/2$ cups chocolate chips, optional

1. Preheat oven to 375°. Empty contents of jar into large bowl.

2. Add eggs, peanut butter, and butter or margarine, softened. Also, if desired, stir in chocolate chips.

3. Beat on low speed to blend.

4. Drop by heaping teaspoonfuls onto ungreased cookie sheet. Bake for 10 to 12 minutes or until edges are lightly browned.

5. Remove from oven and let cookies cool on cookie sheet for 1 minute before transferring to cooling rack. (Makes 4 to $4^1/2$ dozen.)

"*Each friend represents a world in us, a world possibly not born until they arrive, and it is only by this meeting that a new world is born.*"

Anais Nin

Wholesome Peanut Butter Cookies

2 eggs
$^1/_2$ cup crunchy or creamy peanut butter
$^3/_4$ cup (1$^1/_2$ sticks) butter, softened
1$^1/_2$ cups chocolate chips, optional

1. Preheat oven to 375°. Empty contents of jar into large bowl.
2. Add eggs, peanut butter, and softened butter or margarine. Also, if desired, stir in chocolate chips.
3. Beat on low speed to blend.
4. Drop by heaping teaspoonfuls onto ungreased cookie sheet. Bake for 10 to 12 minutes or until edges are lightly browned.
5. Remove from oven and let cookies cool on cookie sheet for 1 minute before transferring to cooling rack. (Makes 4 to 4$^1/_2$ dozen.)

www.cookbookresources.com

Wholesome Peanut Butter Cookies

2 eggs
$^1/_2$ cup crunchy or creamy peanut butter
$^3/_4$ cup (1$^1/_2$ sticks) butter, softened
1$^1/_2$ cups chocolate chips, optional

1. Preheat oven to 375°. Empty contents of jar into large bowl.
2. Add eggs, peanut butter, and softened butter or margarine. Also, if desired, stir in chocolate chips.
3. Beat on low speed to blend.
4. Drop by heaping teaspoonfuls onto ungreased cookie sheet. Bake for 10 to 12 minutes or until edges are lightly browned.
5. Remove from oven and let cookies cool on cookie sheet for 1 minute before transferring to cooling rack. (Makes 4 to 4$^1/_2$ dozen.)

www.cookbookresources.com

Wholesome Peanut Butter Cookies

2 eggs
$^1/_2$ cup crunchy or creamy peanut butter
$^3/_4$ cup (1$^1/_2$ sticks) butter, softened
1$^1/_2$ cups chocolate chips, optional

1. Preheat oven to 375°. Empty contents of jar into large bowl.
2. Add eggs, peanut butter, and softened butter or margarine. Also, if desired, stir in chocolate chips.
3. Beat on low speed to blend.
4. Drop by heaping teaspoonfuls onto ungreased cookie sheet. Bake for 10 to 12 minutes or until edges are lightly browned.
5. Remove from oven and let cookies cool on cookie sheet for 1 minute before transferring to cooling rack. (Makes 4 to 4$^1/_2$ dozen.)

www.cookbookresources.com

Just Because

Wholesome Peanut Butter Cookies

2 eggs
$^1/_2$ cup crunchy or creamy peanut butter
$^3/_4$ cup ($1^1/_2$ sticks) butter, softened
$1^1/_2$ cups chocolate chips, optional

1. Preheat oven to 375°. Empty contents of jar into large bowl.
2. Add eggs, peanut butter, and softened butter or margarine. Also, if desired, stir in chocolate chips.
3. Beat on low speed to blend.
4. Drop by heaping teaspoonfuls onto ungreased cookie sheet. Bake for 10 to 12 minutes or until edges are lightly browned.
5. Remove from oven and let cookies cool on cookie sheet for 1 minute before transferring to cooling rack. (Makes 4 to $4^1/_2$ dozen.)

www.cookbookresources.com

Wholesome Peanut Butter Cookies

2 eggs
$^1/_2$ cup crunchy or creamy peanut butter
$^3/_4$ cup ($1^1/_2$ sticks) butter, softened
$1^1/_2$ cups chocolate chips, optional

1. Preheat oven to 375°. Empty contents of jar into large bowl.
2. Add eggs, peanut butter, and softened butter or margarine. Also, if desired, stir in chocolate chips.
3. Beat on low speed to blend.
4. Drop by heaping teaspoonfuls onto ungreased cookie sheet. Bake for 10 to 12 minutes or until edges are lightly browned.
5. Remove from oven and let cookies cool on cookie sheet for 1 minute before transferring to cooling rack. (Makes 4 to $4^1/_2$ dozen.)

www.cookbookresources.com

Wholesome Peanut Butter Cookies

2 eggs
$^1/_2$ cup crunchy or creamy peanut butter
$^3/_4$ cup ($1^1/_2$ sticks) butter, softened
$1^1/_2$ cups chocolate chips, optional

1. Preheat oven to 375°. Empty contents of jar into large bowl.
2. Add eggs, peanut butter, and softened butter or margarine. Also, if desired, stir in chocolate chips.
3. Beat on low speed to blend.
4. Drop by heaping teaspoonfuls onto ungreased cookie sheet. Bake for 10 to 12 minutes or until edges are lightly browned.
5. Remove from oven and let cookies cool on cookie sheet for 1 minute before transferring to cooling rack. (Makes 4 to $4^1/_2$ dozen.)

www.cookbookresources.com

Happy Birthday

Happy Holidays

Merry Christmas

Orange-Sugar Cookies

Orange-Sugar Cookies

These delicately-flavored sugar cookies have a hint of orange and the distinctive flavor of almonds. They look so pretty in the jar with the alternating bands of orange. To make this an extra-special gift, attach a pretty cookie cutter to the jar with a ribbon.

Ingredients for jar:
1 cup sugar
4 drops red food coloring
4 drops yellow food coloring
3 cups flour
3 tablespoons dried, ground orange peel*
1 teaspoon baking soda
2 teaspoons baking powder
$^1/_2$ cup finely ground almonds, toasted**

Instructions for jar:
1. Place sugar in small bowl. Add red and yellow food coloring and stir well until sugar is evenly colored. (You'll end up with a nice orange color.)
2. In medium bowl, combine flour, orange peel, baking soda and baking powder. Stir well to mix.
3. Place half of sugar in 1-quart jar and smooth over. Spoon half the flour mixture on top and press down, smoothing out top.
4. Place remaining half of sugar over flour layer and press down evenly. Spoon remaining half of flour on top, press down and smooth over.
5. Place toasted almond on top of flour and press down firmly. (It will be a tight squeeze.)
6. Place lid on jar.

Orange-Sugar Cookies
Instructions for baking:

1/2 cup (1 stick) butter, softened
1/2 teaspoon vanilla extract
1 egg
1/2 cup milk

1. Place contents of jar into large bowl. Add butter or margarine, vanilla extract, egg and milk.

2. Beat on low speed to blend. For drop cookies, drop dough by rounded teaspoonful onto ungreased cookie sheet. For rolled cookies, refrigerate dough for a couple of hours to chill (and make it easier to work with). Roll out on lightly floured surface to 1/4" thick. Cut with cookie cutter and place cutouts on ungreased cookie sheet.

3. Bake for 10 minutes. Remove cookies from oven and let cool on cookie sheet for 1 minute, then transfer to cooling rack. (Makes 3 1/2 to 4 dozen.)

* Dried, ground orange peel can be found in the spice section of your grocery store.

* To toast the almonds and bring out their flavor, place the ground nuts on a cookie sheet in a 350° degree oven and bake for about 5 minutes until they're lightly browned. Be sure to check them frequently because they can burn quickly. Let them cool completely before adding them to the jar.

Orange-Sugar Cookies

$1/2$ cup (1 stick) butter, softened
$1/2$ teaspoon vanilla extract
1 egg
$1/2$ cup milk

1. Place contents of jar into large bowl. Add butter or margarine, vanilla extract, egg and milk.
2. Beat on low speed to blend. For drop cookies, drop dough by rounded teaspoonful onto ungreased cookie sheet. For rolled cookies, refrigerate dough for a couple of hours to chill (and make it easier to work with). Roll out on lightly floured surface to $1/4$" thick. Cut with cookie cutter and place cutouts on ungreased cookie sheet.
3. Bake for 10 minutes. Remove cookies from oven and let cool on cookie sheet for 1 minute, then transfer to cooling rack. (Makes $3^1/2$ to 4 dozen.)

Orange-Sugar Cookies

$1/2$ cup (1 stick) butter, softened
$1/2$ teaspoon vanilla extract
1 egg
$1/2$ cup milk

1. Place contents of jar into large bowl. Add butter or margarine, vanilla extract, egg and milk.
2. Beat on low speed to blend. For drop cookies, drop dough by rounded teaspoonful onto ungreased cookie sheet. For rolled cookies, refrigerate dough for a couple of hours to chill (and make it easier to work with). Roll out on lightly floured surface to $1/4$" thick. Cut with cookie cutter and place cutouts on ungreased cookie sheet.
3. Bake for 10 minutes. Remove cookies from oven and let cool on cookie sheet for 1 minute, then transfer to cooling rack. (Makes $3^1/2$ to 4 dozen.)

www.cookbookresources.com

Orange-Sugar Cookies

$1/2$ cup (1 stick) butter, softened
$1/2$ teaspoon vanilla extract
1 egg
$1/2$ cup milk

1. Place contents of jar into large bowl. Add butter or margarine, vanilla extract, egg and milk.
2. Beat on low speed to blend. For drop cookies, drop dough by rounded teaspoonful onto ungreased cookie sheet. For rolled cookies, refrigerate dough for a couple of hours to chill (and make it easier to work with). Roll out on lightly floured surface to $1/4$" thick. Cut with cookie cutter and place cutouts on ungreased cookie sheet.
3. Bake for 10 minutes. Remove cookies from oven and let cool on cookie sheet for 1 minute, then transfer to cooling rack. (Makes $3^1/2$ to 4 dozen.)

www.cookbookresources.com

Thank You

Orange-Sugar Cookies

$^1/_2$ cup (1 stick) butter, softened
$^1/_2$ teaspoon vanilla extract
1 egg
$^1/_2$ cup milk

1. Place contents of jar into large bowl. Add butter or margarine, vanilla extract, egg and milk.
2. Beat on low speed to blend. For drop cookies, drop dough by rounded teaspoonful onto ungreased cookie sheet. For rolled cookies, refrigerate dough for a couple of hours to chill (and make it easier to work with). Roll out on lightly floured surface to $^1/_4$" thick. Cut with cookie cutter and place cutouts on ungreased cookie sheet.
3. Bake for 10 minutes. Remove cookies from oven and let cool on cookie sheet for 1 minute, then transfer to cooling rack. (Makes $3^1/_2$ to 4 dozen.)

www.cookbookresources.com

Orange-Sugar Cookies

$^1/_2$ cup (1 stick) butter, softened
$^1/_2$ teaspoon vanilla extract
1 egg
$^1/_2$ cup milk

1. Place contents of jar into large bowl. Add butter or margarine, vanilla extract, egg and milk.
2. Beat on low speed to blend. For drop cookies, drop dough by rounded teaspoonful onto ungreased cookie sheet. For rolled cookies, refrigerate dough for a couple of hours to chill (and make it easier to work with). Roll out on lightly floured surface to $^1/_4$" thick. Cut with cookie cutter and place cutouts on ungreased cookie sheet.
3. Bake for 10 minutes. Remove cookies from oven and let cool on cookie sheet for 1 minute, then transfer to cooling rack. (Makes $3^1/_2$ to 4 dozen.)

www.cookbookresources.com

Orange-Sugar Cookies

$^1/_2$ cup (1 stick) butter, softened
$^1/_2$ teaspoon vanilla extract
1 egg
$^1/_2$ cup milk

1. Place contents of jar into large bowl. Add butter or margarine, vanilla extract, egg and milk.
2. Beat on low speed to blend. For drop cookies, drop dough by rounded teaspoonful onto ungreased cookie sheet. For rolled cookies, refrigerate dough for a couple of hours to chill (and make it easier to work with). Roll out on lightly floured surface to $^1/_4$" thick. Cut with cookie cutter and place cutouts on ungreased cookie sheet.
3. Bake for 10 minutes. Remove cookies from oven and let cool on cookie sheet for 1 minute, then transfer to cooling rack. (Makes $3^1/_2$ to 4 dozen.)

www.cookbookresources.com

Happy Birthday

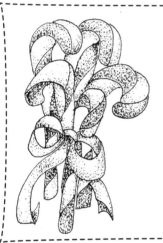

Happy Holidays

Merry Christmas!

Mocha-Chocolate Chip Cookies

Mocha-Chocolate Chip Cookies

These dark, rich chocolate, mocha-flavor cookies
are studded with chocolate chips.

Ingredients for jar:

$^3/_4$ cup packed dark brown sugar
$^1/_2$ cup sugar
$^1/_4$ cup cocoa
2 tablespoons instant coffee
$1^3/_4$ cups flour
1 teaspoon baking soda
1 teaspoon baking powder
$^1/_4$ teaspoon salt
1 cup semi-sweet chocolate chips

Instructions for jar:

1. Place brown sugar in 1-quart jar and press down firmly and evenly.
2. Pour sugar on top and smooth over.
3. In medium bowl, combine cocoa, coffee, flour, cocoa, baking soda, baking powder and salt. Stir well until evenly colored. Spoon flour mixture into jar in several additions, pressing down with each addition. When entire mixture has been added, smooth over top.
4. Gently sprinkle chocolate chips on top of flour mixture and press down firmly.
5. Place lid on jar.

Mocha-Chocolate Chip Cookies
Instructions for baking:

$^3/_4$ cup ($1^1/_2$ sticks) butter, softened
1 egg, slightly beaten
1 teaspoon vanilla

1. Preheat oven to 350°. Empty contents of jar into large bowl.

2. Add butter or margarine, egg and vanilla.

3. Beat on low speed to blend.

4. Drop by heaping teaspoonfuls onto ungreased cookie sheet. Bake for 10 to 12 minutes. Remove from oven and let cookies cool on cookie sheet for 1 minute, then transfer to cooling rack. (Makes 3 to $3^1/_2$ dozen.)

"A friend is someone who knows the song in your heat and can sing it back to you when you have forgotten the words."

Anonymous

Mocha-Chocolate Chip Cookies

$3/4$ cup ($1^1/_2$ sticks) butter, softened
1 egg, slightly beaten
1 teaspoon vanilla

1. Preheat oven to 350°. Empty contents of jar into large bowl.
2. Add butter or margarine, egg and vanilla.
3. Beat on low speed to blend.
4. Drop by heaping teaspoonfuls onto ungreased cookie sheet. Bake for 10 to 12 minutes. Remove from oven and let cookies cool on cookie sheet for 1 minute, then transfer to cooling rack. (Makes 3 to $3^1/_2$ dozen.)

www.cookbookresources.com

Mocha-Chocolate Chip Cookies

$3/4$ cup ($1^1/_2$ sticks) butter, softened
1 egg, slightly beaten
1 teaspoon vanilla

1. Preheat oven to 350°. Empty contents of jar into large bowl.
2. Add butter or margarine, egg and vanilla.
3. Beat on low speed to blend.
4. Drop by heaping teaspoonfuls onto ungreased cookie sheet. Bake for 10 to 12 minutes. Remove from oven and let cookies cool on cookie sheet for 1 minute, then transfer to cooling rack. (Makes 3 to $3^1/_2$ dozen.)

www.cookbookresources.com

Mocha-Chocolate Chip Cookies

$3/4$ cup ($1^1/_2$ sticks) butter, softened
1 egg, slightly beaten
1 teaspoon vanilla

1. Preheat oven to 350°. Empty contents of jar into large bowl.
2. Add butter or margarine, egg and vanilla.
3. Beat on low speed to blend.
4. Drop by heaping teaspoonfuls onto ungreased cookie sheet. Bake for 10 to 12 minutes. Remove from oven and let cookies cool on cookie sheet for 1 minute, then transfer to cooling rack. (Makes 3 to $3^1/_2$ dozen.)

www.cookbookresources.com

You're the Best

For My Good Friend

Mocha-Chocolate Chip Cookies

$^3/_4$ cup ($1^1/_2$ sticks) butter, softened
1 egg, slightly beaten
1 teaspoon vanilla

1. Preheat oven to 350°. Empty contents of jar into large bowl.
2. Add butter or margarine, egg and vanilla.
3. Beat on low speed to blend.
4. Drop by heaping teaspoonfuls onto ungreased cookie sheet. Bake for 10 to 12 minutes. Remove from oven and let cookies cool on cookie sheet for 1 minute, then transfer to cooling rack. (Makes 3 to $3^1/_2$ dozen.)

Mocha-Chocolate Chip Cookies

$^3/_4$ cup ($1^1/_2$ sticks) butter, softened
1 egg, slightly beaten
1 teaspoon vanilla

1. Preheat oven to 350°. Empty contents of jar into large bowl.
2. Add butter or margarine, egg and vanilla.
3. Beat on low speed to blend.
4. Drop by heaping teaspoonfuls onto ungreased cookie sheet. Bake for 10 to 12 minutes. Remove from oven and let cookies cool on cookie sheet for 1 minute, then transfer to cooling rack. (Makes 3 to $3^1/_2$ dozen.)

Mocha-Chocolate Chip Cookies

$^3/_4$ cup ($1^1/_2$ sticks) butter, softened
1 egg, slightly beaten
1 teaspoon vanilla

1. Preheat oven to 350°. Empty contents of jar into large bowl.
2. Add butter or margarine, egg and vanilla.
3. Beat on low speed to blend.
4. Drop by heaping teaspoonfuls onto ungreased cookie sheet. Bake for 10 to 12 minutes. Remove from oven and let cookies cool on cookie sheet for 1 minute, then transfer to cooling rack. (Makes 3 to $3^1/_2$ dozen.)

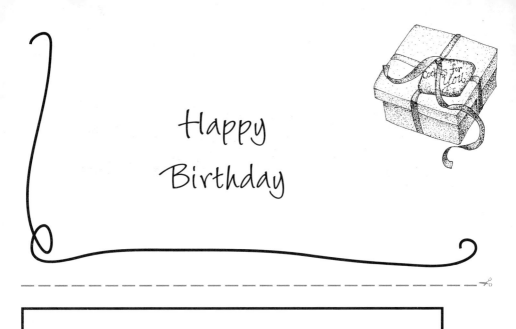

Happy
Birthday

Happy Holidays

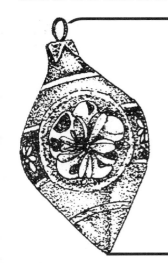

Merry Christmas

Rich Date and Walnut Cookies

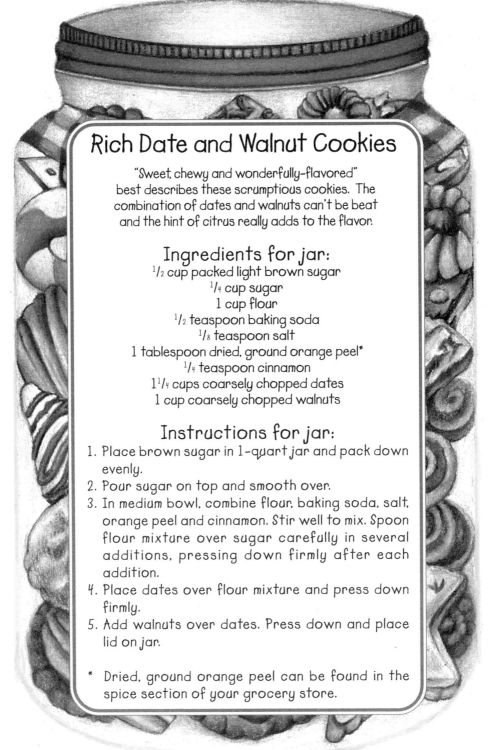

Rich Date and Walnut Cookies

"Sweet, chewy and wonderfully-flavored" best describes these scrumptious cookies. The combination of dates and walnuts can't be beat and the hint of citrus really adds to the flavor.

Ingredients for jar:

$1/2$ cup packed light brown sugar
$1/4$ cup sugar
1 cup flour
$1/2$ teaspoon baking soda
$1/8$ teaspoon salt
1 tablespoon dried, ground orange peel*
$1/4$ teaspoon cinnamon
$1^1/4$ cups coarsely chopped dates
1 cup coarsely chopped walnuts

Instructions for jar:

1. Place brown sugar in 1-quart jar and pack down evenly.
2. Pour sugar on top and smooth over.
3. In medium bowl, combine flour, baking soda, salt, orange peel and cinnamon. Stir well to mix. Spoon flour mixture over sugar carefully in several additions, pressing down firmly after each addition.
4. Place dates over flour mixture and press down firmly.
5. Add walnuts over dates. Press down and place lid on jar.

* Dried, ground orange peel can be found in the spice section of your grocery store.

Rich Date and Walnut Cookies
Instructions for baking:

¹/₂ cup (1 stick) butter, softened
1 egg

1. Preheat oven to 350°. Empty contents of jar into large bowl.

2. Add butter or margarine and egg.

3. Beat on low speed or by hand until well mixed.

4. Drop by rounded teaspoonfuls onto ungreased cookie sheet. Bake for 10 to 12 minutes.

5. Remove from oven and let cookies cool on cookie sheet for 1 minute, then transfer to cooling rack. (Makes 2¹/₂ to 3 dozen.)

"*Some people come into our lives and quickly go. Some stay for awhile and leave footprints on our hearts. And we are never, ever the same.*"

Anonymous

Rich Date and Walnut Cookies

$^1/_2$ cup (1 stick) butter, softened
1 egg

1. Preheat oven to 350°. Empty contents of jar into large bowl.
2. Add butter or margarine and egg.
3. Beat on low speed or by hand until well mixed.
4. Drop by rounded teaspoonfuls onto ungreased cookie sheet. Bake for 10 to 12 minutes.
5. Remove from oven and let cookies cool on cookie sheet for 1 minute, then transfer to cooling rack. (Makes $2^1/_2$ to 3 dozen.)

www.cookbookresources.com

- ✂

Rich Date and Walnut Cookies

$^1/_2$ cup (1 stick) butter, softened
1 egg

1. Preheat oven to 350°. Empty contents of jar into large bowl.
2. Add butter or margarine and egg.
3. Beat on low speed or by hand until well mixed.
4. Drop by rounded teaspoonfuls onto ungreased cookie sheet. Bake for 10 to 12 minutes.
5. Remove from oven and let cookies cool on cookie sheet for 1 minute, then transfer to cooling rack. (Makes $2^1/_2$ to 3 dozen.)

www.cookbookresources.com

- ✂

Rich Date and Walnut Cookies

$^1/_2$ cup (1 stick) butter, softened
1 egg

1. Preheat oven to 350°. Empty contents of jar into large bowl.
2. Add butter or margarine and egg.
3. Beat on low speed or by hand until well mixed.
4. Drop by rounded teaspoonfuls onto ungreased cookie sheet. Bake for 10 to 12 minutes.
5. Remove from oven and let cookies cool on cookie sheet for 1 minute, then transfer to cooling rack. (Makes $2^1/_2$ to 3 dozen.)

www.cookbookresources.com

You're a Doll

Rich Date and Walnut Cookies

¹/₂ cup (1 stick) butter, softened
1 egg

1. Preheat oven to 350°. Empty contents of jar into large bowl.
2. Add butter or margarine and egg.
3. Beat on low speed or by hand until well mixed.
4. Drop by rounded teaspoonfuls onto ungreased cookie sheet. Bake for 10 to 12 minutes.
5. Remove from oven and let cookies cool on cookie sheet for 1 minute, then transfer to cooling rack. (Makes $2^1/_2$ to 3 dozen.)

www.cookbookresources.com

Rich Date and Walnut Cookies

¹/₂ cup (1 stick) butter, softened
1 egg

1. Preheat oven to 350°. Empty contents of jar into large bowl.
2. Add butter or margarine and egg.
3. Beat on low speed or by hand until well mixed.
4. Drop by rounded teaspoonfuls onto ungreased cookie sheet. Bake for 10 to 12 minutes.
5. Remove from oven and let cookies cool on cookie sheet for 1 minute, then transfer to cooling rack. (Makes $2^1/_2$ to 3 dozen.)

www.cookbookresources.com

Rich Date and Walnut Cookies

¹/₂ cup (1 stick) butter, softened
1 egg

1. Preheat oven to 350°. Empty contents of jar into large bowl.
2. Add butter or margarine and egg.
3. Beat on low speed or by hand until well mixed.
4. Drop by rounded teaspoonfuls onto ungreased cookie sheet. Bake for 10 to 12 minutes.
5. Remove from oven and let cookies cool on cookie sheet for 1 minute, then transfer to cooling rack. (Makes $2^1/_2$ to 3 dozen.)

www.cookbookresources.com

Happy Birthday

Happy Holidays

Merry Christmas

Lightly Spiced Raisin Cookies

Lightly Spiced Raisin Cookies

These delicate cookies have a hint of spices and are full of raisins. They're tender and crispy on the edges, but soft in the middle. They would make a wonderful house-warming gift.

Ingredients for jar:
1 cup sugar
2 cups flour
$1/2$ teaspoon salt
$1/2$ teaspoon ground cloves
1 teaspoon ginger
1 teaspoon cinnamon
3 teaspoons baking soda
1 cup raisins

Instructions for jar:
1. Pour sugar into 1-quart jar and smooth over to make even.
2. In medium bowl, combine flour, salt, cloves, ginger, cinnamon and baking soda. Stir to mix thoroughly. Gently spoon mixture over sugar and press down lightly.
3. Carefully add raisins on top of flour. Place lid on jar.

Lightly Spiced Raisin Cookies

Instructions for baking:

1 egg, slightly beaten
$^3/_4$ cup ($1^1/_2$ sticks) butter, softened
Several tablespoons sugar

1. Preheat oven to 350°. Empty contents of jar into large bowl. Add egg and butter or margarine.

2. Beat on low speed or by hand to blend. Roll dough into balls 1-inch wide and place on ungreased cookie sheet.

3. Flatten with bottom of a glass dipped in sugar.

4. Bake for 10 to 12 minutes until edges are lightly browned. Remove from oven and let cookies cool on cookie sheet for 1 minute before transferring to cooling rack. (Makes $3^1/_2$ to 4 dozen.)

"A friend is a gift you give yourself."
Robert Louis Stevenson

Lightly Spiced Raisin Cookies

1 egg, slightly beaten
$^3/_4$ cup ($1^1/_2$ sticks) butter, softened
Several tablespoons sugar

1. Preheat oven to 350°. Empty contents of jar into large bowl. Add egg and butter or margarine.
2. Beat on low speed or by hand to blend. Roll dough into balls 1-inch wide and place on ungreased cookie sheet.
3. Flatten with bottom of a glass dipped in sugar.
4. Bake for 10 to 12 minutes until edges are lightly browned. Remove from oven and let cookies cool on cookie sheet for 1 minute before transferring to cooling rack. (Makes $3^1/_2$ to 4 dozen.)

www.cookbookresources.com

Lightly Spiced Raisin Cookies

1 egg, slightly beaten
$^3/_4$ cup ($1^1/_2$ sticks) butter, softened
Several tablespoons sugar

1. Preheat oven to 350°. Empty contents of jar into large bowl. Add egg and butter or margarine.
2. Beat on low speed or by hand to blend. Roll dough into balls 1-inch wide and place on ungreased cookie sheet.
3. Flatten with bottom of a glass dipped in sugar.
4. Bake for 10 to 12 minutes until edges are lightly browned. Remove from oven and let cookies cool on cookie sheet for 1 minute before transferring to cooling rack. (Makes $3^1/_2$ to 4 dozen.)

www.cookbookresources.com

Lightly Spiced Raisin Cookies

1 egg, slightly beaten
$^3/_4$ cup ($1^1/_2$ sticks) butter, softened
Several tablespoons sugar

1. Preheat oven to 350°. Empty contents of jar into large bowl. Add egg and butter or margarine.
2. Beat on low speed or by hand to blend. Roll dough into balls 1-inch wide and place on ungreased cookie sheet.
3. Flatten with bottom of a glass dipped in sugar.
4. Bake for 10 to 12 minutes until edges are lightly browned. Remove from oven and let cookies cool on cookie sheet for 1 minute before transferring to cooling rack. (Makes $3^1/_2$ to 4 dozen.)

www.cookbookresources.com

Thinking of You

Lightly Spiced Raisin Cookies

1 egg, slightly beaten
$^3/_4$ cup (1$^1/_2$ sticks) butter, softened
several tablespoons sugar

1. Preheat oven to 350°. Empty contents of jar into large bowl. Add egg and butter or margarine.
2. Beat on low speed or by hand to blend. Roll dough into balls 1-inch wide and place on ungreased cookie sheet.
3. Flatten with bottom of a glass dipped in sugar.
4. Bake for 10 to 12 minutes until edges are lightly browned. Remove from oven and let cookies cool on cookie sheet for 1 minute before transferring to cooling rack. (Makes 3$^1/_2$ to 4 dozen.)

Lightly Spiced Raisin Cookies

1 egg, slightly beaten
$^3/_4$ cup (1$^1/_2$ sticks) butter, softened
several tablespoons sugar

1. Preheat oven to 350°. Empty contents of jar into large bowl. Add egg and butter or margarine.
2. Beat on low speed or by hand to blend. Roll dough into balls 1-inch wide and place on ungreased cookie sheet.
3. Flatten with bottom of a glass dipped in sugar.
4. Bake for 10 to 12 minutes until edges are lightly browned. Remove from oven and let cookies cool on cookie sheet for 1 minute before transferring to cooling rack. (Makes 3$^1/_2$ to 4 dozen.)

www.cookbookresources.com

Lightly Spiced Raisin Cookies

1 egg, slightly beaten
$^3/_4$ cup (1$^1/_2$ sticks) butter, softened
several tablespoons sugar

1. Preheat oven to 350°. Empty contents of jar into large bowl. Add egg and butter or margarine.
2. Beat on low speed or by hand to blend. Roll dough into balls 1-inch wide and place on ungreased cookie sheet.
3. Flatten with bottom of a glass dipped in sugar.
4. Bake for 10 to 12 minutes until edges are lightly browned. Remove from oven and let cookies cool on cookie sheet for 1 minute before transferring to cooling rack. (Makes 3$^1/_2$ to 4 dozen.)

www.cookbookresources.com

Happy Birthday

Happy Holidays

Merry Christmas

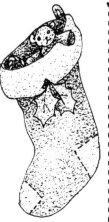

Peanutty Clusters

Peanutty Clusters

These crispy cookies burst with peanut flavor, which is enhanced by butterscotch candies.

Ingredients for jar:
$1/2$ cup packed light brown sugar
$1/2$ cup sugar
$3/4$ cup cocktail peanuts
$1 1/2$ cups flour
$3/4$ teaspoon baking soda
$1/2$ teaspoon baking powder
$1/4$ teaspoon salt
1 cup butterscotch-flavored baking chips
$1/2$ cup coconut

Instructions for jar:
1. Place brown sugar in 1-quart jar and press down evenly.
2. Pour sugar evenly over brown sugar.
3. Sprinkle peanuts over sugar and press down.
4. In medium bowl, combine flour, baking soda, baking powder and salt. Mix well. Pour half of mixture over peanuts, pressing down firmly.
5. Pour butterscotch chips over flour in jar and top with remaining flour.
6. Place coconut on top of flour and press down firmly. Place lid on jar.

Peanutty Clusters

Instructions for baking:

$^1/_2$ cup (1 stick) butter, softened
$^1/_2$ cup creamy peanut butter
1 egg
Several tablespoons sugar

1. Preheat oven to 375°. Empty contents of jar into large bowl and add butter or margarine, peanut butter and egg.

2. Beat on low speed or by hand to blend. Roll heaping teaspoonfuls of dough into balls and place 3 inches apart on ungreased cookie sheet. Flatten with bottom of glass dipped in sugar.

3. Bake for 10 to 12 minutes or until edges are browned. Remove from oven and let cookies cool on cookie sheet for 1 minute before transferring to cooling rack. (Makes about 4 dozen.)

"*There are no such things as strangers, only friends we haven't met yet.*"
Anonymous

Peanutty Clusters

½ cup (1 stick) butter, softened
½ cup creamy peanut butter
1 egg
Several tablespoons sugar

1. Preheat oven to 375°. Empty contents of jar into large bowl and add butter or margarine, peanut butter and egg.
2. Beat on low speed or by hand to blend. Roll heaping teaspoonfuls of dough into balls and place 3 inches apart on ungreased cookie sheet. Flatten with bottom of glass dipped in sugar.
3. Bake for 10 to 12 minutes or until edges are browned. Remove from oven and let cookies cool on cookie sheet for 1 minute before transferring to cooling rack. (Makes about 4 dozen.)

www.cookbookresources.com

Peanutty Clusters

½ cup (1 stick) butter, softened
½ cup creamy peanut butter
1 egg
Several tablespoons sugar

1. Preheat oven to 375°. Empty contents of jar into large bowl and add butter or margarine, peanut butter and egg.
2. Beat on low speed or by hand to blend. Roll heaping teaspoonfuls of dough into balls and place 3 inches apart on ungreased cookie sheet. Flatten with bottom of glass dipped in sugar.
3. Bake for 10 to 12 minutes or until edges are browned. Remove from oven and let cookies cool on cookie sheet for 1 minute before transferring to cooling rack. (Makes about 4 dozen.)

www.cookbookresources.com

Peanutty Clusters

½ cup (1 stick) butter, softened
½ cup creamy peanut butter
1 egg
Several tablespoons sugar

1. Preheat oven to 375°. Empty contents of jar into large bowl and add butter or margarine, peanut butter and egg.
2. Beat on low speed or by hand to blend. Roll heaping teaspoonfuls of dough into balls and place 3 inches apart on ungreased cookie sheet. Flatten with bottom of glass dipped in sugar.
3. Bake for 10 to 12 minutes or until edges are browned. Remove from oven and let cookies cool on cookie sheet for 1 minute before transferring to cooling rack. (Makes about 4 dozen.)

www.cookbookresources.com

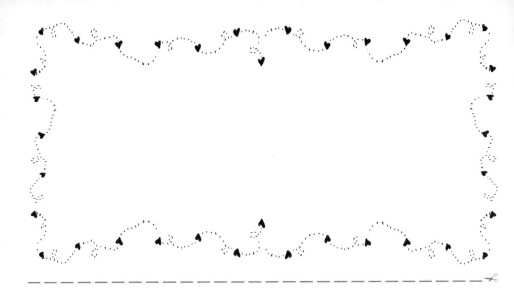

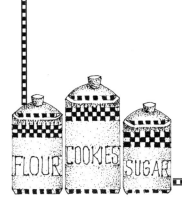

You're a Pal

Peanutty Clusters

½ cup (1 stick) butter, softened
½ cup creamy peanut butter
1 egg
Several tablespoons sugar

1. Preheat oven to 375°. Empty contents of jar into large bowl and add butter or margarine, peanut butter and egg.
2. Beat on low speed or by hand to blend. Roll heaping teaspoonfuls of dough into balls and place 3 inches apart on ungreased cookie sheet. Flatten with bottom of glass dipped in sugar.
3. Bake for 10 to 12 minutes or until edges are browned. Remove from oven and let cookies cool on cookie sheet for 1 minute before transferring to cooling rack. (Makes about 4 dozen.)

www.cookbookresources.com

Peanutty Clusters

½ cup (1 stick) butter, softened
½ cup creamy peanut butter
1 egg
Several tablespoons sugar

1. Preheat oven to 375°. Empty contents of jar into large bowl and add butter or margarine, peanut butter and egg.
2. Beat on low speed or by hand to blend. Roll heaping teaspoonfuls of dough into balls and place 3 inches apart on ungreased cookie sheet. Flatten with bottom of glass dipped in sugar.
3. Bake for 10 to 12 minutes or until edges are browned. Remove from oven and let cookies cool on cookie sheet for 1 minute before transferring to cooling rack. (Makes about 4 dozen.)

www.cookbookresources.com

Peanutty Clusters

½ cup (1 stick) butter, softened
½ cup creamy peanut butter
1 egg
Several tablespoons sugar

1. Preheat oven to 375°. Empty contents of jar into large bowl and add butter or margarine, peanut butter and egg.
2. Beat on low speed or by hand to blend. Roll heaping teaspoonfuls of dough into balls and place 3 inches apart on ungreased cookie sheet. Flatten with bottom of glass dipped in sugar.
3. Bake for 10 to 12 minutes or until edges are browned. Remove from oven and let cookies cool on cookie sheet for 1 minute before transferring to cooling rack. (Makes about 4 dozen.)

www.cookbookresources.com

Happy Birthday

Happy Holidays

Merry Christmas

Banana Nut Cookies

Banana Nut Cookies

These hearty, blonde cookies are cake-like in texture and full of banana flavor.

Ingredients for jar:

$1^{1}/_{2}$ cups flour
1 teaspoon baking powder
$^{1}/_{4}$ teaspoon baking soda
$^{1}/_{2}$ teaspoon salt
1 cup sugar
1 teaspoon cinnamon
$^{1}/_{4}$ teaspoon nutmeg
$1^{1}/_{2}$ cups quick-cooking oats
$^{1}/_{3}$ cup finely chopped walnuts

Instructions for jar:

1. In small bowl, combine flour with baking powder, baking soda and salt. Mix well. Spoon into 1-quart jar and press down.
2. In another bowl, combine sugar with cinnamon and nutmeg. Stir until mixed and evenly-colored. Pour sugar mixture over flour and even out the surface.
3. Add the oats on top of sugar, pressing down firmly.
4. Pour nuts over oats and press down. Place lid on jar.

Banana Nut Cookies

Instructions for baking:

$1/2$ cup (1 stick) butter, softened
2 eggs
1 cup mashed, ripe bananas

1. Preheat oven to 375°. Add butter or margarine, eggs and bananas.

2. Beat on low speed or by hand to blend. Drop by heaping teaspoonfuls onto lightly greased cookie sheet. Bake for 12 minutes.

3. Remove from oven and let cookies cool on cookie sheet for 1 minute, then transfer to cooling rack. (Makes $3 1/2$ to 4 dozen.)

"My best friend is the one that brings out the best in me."

Henry Ford

68

Banana Nut Cookies

$^1/_2$ cup (1 stick) butter, softened
2 eggs
1 cup mashed, ripe bananas

1. Preheat oven to 375°. Add butter or margarine, eggs and bananas.
2. Beat on low speed or by hand to blend. Drop by heaping teaspoonfuls onto lightly greased cookie sheet. Bake for 12 minutes.
3. Remove from oven and let cookies cool on cookie sheet for 1 minute, then transfer to cooling rack. (Makes $3^1/_2$ to 4 dozen.)

Banana Nut Cookies

$^1/_2$ cup (1 stick) butter, softened
2 eggs
1 cup mashed, ripe bananas

1. Preheat oven to 375°. Add butter or margarine, eggs and bananas.
2. Beat on low speed or by hand to blend. Drop by heaping teaspoonfuls onto lightly greased cookie sheet. Bake for 12 minutes.
3. Remove from oven and let cookies cool on cookie sheet for 1 minute, then transfer to cooling rack. (Makes $3^1/_2$ to 4 dozen.)

Banana Nut Cookies

$^1/_2$ cup (1 stick) butter, softened
2 eggs
1 cup mashed, ripe bananas

1. Preheat oven to 375°. Add butter or margarine, eggs and bananas.
2. Beat on low speed or by hand to blend. Drop by heaping teaspoonfuls onto lightly greased cookie sheet. Bake for 12 minutes.
3. Remove from oven and let cookies cool on cookie sheet for 1 minute, then transfer to cooling rack. (Makes $3^1/_2$ to 4 dozen.)

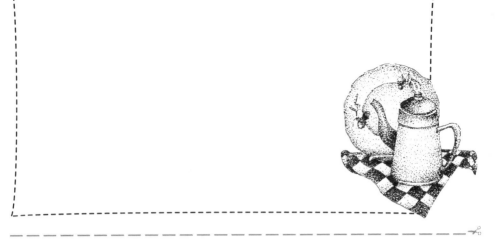

Best Wishes

Banana Nut Cookies

$^1/_2$ cup (1 stick) butter, softened
2 eggs
1 cup mashed, ripe bananas

1. Preheat oven to 375°. Add butter or margarine, eggs and bananas.
2. Beat on low speed or by hand to blend. Drop by heaping teaspoonfuls onto lightly greased cookie sheet. Bake for 12 minutes.
3. Remove from oven and let cookies cool on cookie sheet for 1 minute, then transfer to cooling rack. (Makes $3^1/_2$ to 4 dozen.)

Banana Nut Cookies

$^1/_2$ cup (1 stick) butter, softened
2 eggs
1 cup mashed, ripe bananas

1. Preheat oven to 375°. Add butter or margarine, eggs and bananas.
2. Beat on low speed or by hand to blend. Drop by heaping teaspoonfuls onto lightly greased cookie sheet. Bake for 12 minutes.
3. Remove from oven and let cookies cool on cookie sheet for 1 minute, then transfer to cooling rack. (Makes $3^1/_2$ to 4 dozen.)

Banana Nut Cookies

$^1/_2$ cup (1 stick) butter, softened
2 eggs
1 cup mashed, ripe bananas

1. Preheat oven to 375°. Add butter or margarine, eggs and bananas.
2. Beat on low speed or by hand to blend. Drop by heaping teaspoonfuls onto lightly greased cookie sheet. Bake for 12 minutes.
3. Remove from oven and let cookies cool on cookie sheet for 1 minute, then transfer to cooling rack. (Makes $3^1/_2$ to 4 dozen.)

Happy Birthday

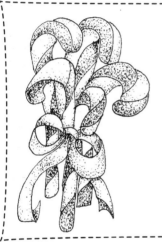

Happy Holidays

Merry Christmas!

Buttermilk-Raisin Cookies

Buttermilk-Raisin Cookies

A light, cake-like cookie with the flavor of buttermilk pie, these little treats are perfect with a cup of steaming hot tea. They have a delicate flavor complemented by the sweet raisins sprinkled throughout.

Ingredients for jar:
1 cup packed light brown sugar
2 cups flour
$1/2$ teaspoon baking powder
$1/2$ teaspoon baking soda
$1/4$ teaspoon salt
1 tablespoon dried, ground lemon peel*
1 cup raisins
$1/2$ cup coarsely chopped walnuts

Instructions for jar:
1. Place brown sugar in 1-quart jar and press down firmly, making sure surface is even.
2. In medium bowl, combine flour, baking powder, baking soda, salt and lemon peel. Stir well to mix. Spoon mixture over brown sugar, pressing down firmly and smoothing out the top.
3. Pour raisins on top of flour mixture and press down.
4. Add walnuts on top of raisins, pressing down firmly. Place lid on jar.

*Dried, ground lemon peel can be found in the spice section of the grocery store.

Buttermilk-Raisin Cookies
Instructions for baking:

$^1/_2$ cup (1 stick) butter, softened
1 egg
$^3/_4$ cup buttermilk

1. Preheat oven to 375°. In large bowl, combine contents of jar with butter or margarine, egg and buttermilk.

2. Beat on low speed to blend (cookie dough will be soft like a batter). Drop by tablespoons onto lightly greased cookie sheet.

3. Bake for 10 to 11 minutes or until edges are lightly browned. Remove from oven and let cookies cool on cookie sheet for 1 minute, then transfer to cooling rack. (Makes 3 to $3^1/_2$ dozen.)

"My friends are my estate."
-*Emily Dickinson*

Buttermilk-Raisin Cookies

$^1/_2$ cup (1 stick) butter, softened
1 egg
$^3/_4$ cup buttermilk

1. Preheat oven to 375°. In large bowl, combine contents of jar with butter or margarine, egg and buttermilk.
2. Beat on low speed to blend (cookie dough will be soft like a batter). Drop by tablespoons onto lightly greased cookie sheet.
3. Bake for 10 to 11 minutes or until edges are lightly browned. Remove from oven and let cookies cool on cookie sheet for 1 minute, then transfer to cooling rack. (Makes 3 to $3^1/_2$ dozen.)

www.cookbookresources.com

Buttermilk-Raisin Cookies

$^1/_2$ cup (1 stick) butter, softened
1 egg
$^3/_4$ cup buttermilk

1. Preheat oven to 375°. In large bowl, combine contents of jar with butter or margarine, egg and buttermilk.
2. Beat on low speed to blend (cookie dough will be soft like a batter). Drop by tablespoons onto lightly greased cookie sheet.
3. Bake for 10 to 11 minutes or until edges are lightly browned. Remove from oven and let cookies cool on cookie sheet for 1 minute, then transfer to cooling rack. (Makes 3 to $3^1/_2$ dozen.)

www.cookbookresources.com

Buttermilk-Raisin Cookies

$^1/_2$ cup (1 stick) butter, softened
1 egg
$^3/_4$ cup buttermilk

1. Preheat oven to 375°. In large bowl, combine contents of jar with butter or margarine, egg and buttermilk.
2. Beat on low speed to blend (cookie dough will be soft like a batter). Drop by tablespoons onto lightly greased cookie sheet.
3. Bake for 10 to 11 minutes or until edges are lightly browned. Remove from oven and let cookies cool on cookie sheet for 1 minute, then transfer to cooling rack. (Makes 3 to $3^1/_2$ dozen.)

www.cookbookresources.com

Just Because

Buttermilk-Raisin Cookies

$1/2$ cup (1 stick) butter, softened
1 egg
$3/4$ cup buttermilk

1. Preheat oven to 375°. In large bowl, combine contents of jar with butter or margarine, egg and buttermilk.
2. Beat on low speed to blend (cookie dough will be soft like a batter). Drop by tablespoons onto lightly greased cookie sheet.
3. Bake for 10 to 11 minutes or until edges are lightly browned. Remove from oven and let cookies cool on cookie sheet for 1 minute, then transfer to cooling rack. (Makes 3 to $3^1/2$ dozen.)

www.cookbookresources.com

Buttermilk-Raisin Cookies

$1/2$ cup (1 stick) butter, softened
1 egg
$3/4$ cup buttermilk

1. Preheat oven to 375°. In large bowl, combine contents of jar with butter or margarine, egg and buttermilk.
2. Beat on low speed to blend (cookie dough will be soft like a batter). Drop by tablespoons onto lightly greased cookie sheet.
3. Bake for 10 to 11 minutes or until edges are lightly browned. Remove from oven and let cookies cool on cookie sheet for 1 minute, then transfer to cooling rack. (Makes 3 to $3^1/2$ dozen.)

www.cookbookresources.com

Buttermilk-Raisin Cookies

$1/2$ cup (1 stick) butter, softened
1 egg
$3/4$ cup buttermilk

1. Preheat oven to 375°. In large bowl, combine contents of jar with butter or margarine, egg and buttermilk.
2. Beat on low speed to blend (cookie dough will be soft like a batter). Drop by tablespoons onto lightly greased cookie sheet.
3. Bake for 10 to 11 minutes or until edges are lightly browned. Remove from oven and let cookies cool on cookie sheet for 1 minute, then transfer to cooling rack. (Makes 3 to $3^1/2$ dozen.)

www.cookbookresources.com

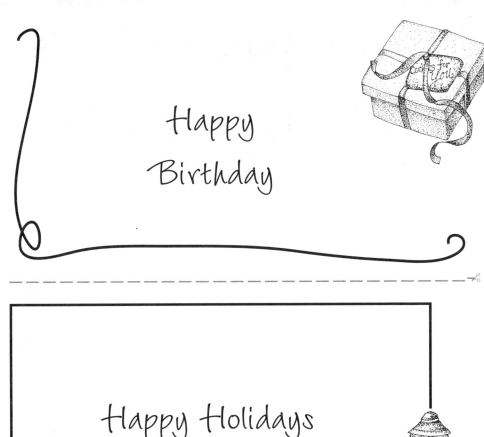

Happy
Birthday

Happy Holidays

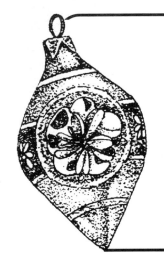

Merry Christmas

Holiday Honey-Spice Cookies

Holiday Honey-Spice Cookies

These golden-colored crispy cookies are sweet and full of citrus and spice flavor. They make a lovely gift at the holidays.

Ingredients for jar:
1 cup sugar
1 cup packed light brown sugar
$2^1/_2$ cups flour
1 teaspoon cinnamon
$^1/_2$ teaspoon ground cloves
$^1/_8$ teaspoon ground nutmeg
1 tablespoon dried, ground lemon peel*
1 tablespoon dried, ground orange peel*
1 teaspoon baking soda

Instructions for jar:
1. Pour sugar evenly in 1-quart jar.
2. Place brown sugar on top and pack down evenly.
3. In medium bowl, combine flour with remaining ingredients and mix well. Spoon flour mixture over brown sugar in jar and press down firmly after each addition.
4. Place lid on jar.

*Dried, ground lemon peel and orange peel can be found in the spice section of the grocery store.

Holiday Honey-Spice Cookies
Instructions for baking:

$^1/_2$ cup honey
$^1/_4$ cup ($^1/_2$ stick) butter, softened
1 egg
2 tablespoons milk

1. Preheat oven to 350°. Empty contents of jar into large mixing bowl. Add honey, butter or margarine, egg and milk.

2. Beat on low speed or by hand until dough is completely mixed.

3. Roll pieces of dough into 1-inch balls and place 3 inches apart on lightly greased cookie sheet.

4. Bake for 10 to 12 minutes or until cookies are golden brown. Remove from oven and let cookies cool on cookie sheet for 1 minute, then transfer to cooling rack. (Makes $3^1/_2$ to 4 dozen.)

"Friends are the most important ingredient in this recipe of life."

Holiday Honey-Spice Cookies

$1/2$ cup honey
$1/4$ cup ($1/2$ stick) butter, softened
1 egg
2 tablespoons milk

1. Preheat oven to 350°. Empty contents of jar into large mixing bowl. Add honey, butter or margarine, egg and milk.
2. Beat on low speed or by hand until dough is completely mixed.
3. Roll pieces of dough into 1-inch balls and place 3 inches apart on lightly greased cookie sheet.
4. Bake for 10 to 12 minutes or until cookies are golden brown. Remove from oven and let cookies cool on cookie sheet for 1 minute, then transfer to cooling rack. (Makes $3^1/2$ to 4 dozen.)

www.cookbookresources.com

Holiday Honey-Spice Cookies

$1/2$ cup honey
$1/4$ cup ($1/2$ stick) butter, softened
1 egg
2 tablespoons milk

1. Preheat oven to 350°. Empty contents of jar into large mixing bowl. Add honey, butter or margarine, egg and milk.
2. Beat on low speed or by hand until dough is completely mixed.
3. Roll pieces of dough into 1-inch balls and place 3 inches apart on lightly greased cookie sheet.
4. Bake for 10 to 12 minutes or until cookies are golden brown. Remove from oven and let cookies cool on cookie sheet for 1 minute, then transfer to cooling rack. (Makes $3^1/2$ to 4 dozen.)

www.cookbookresources.com

Holiday Honey-Spice Cookies

$1/2$ cup honey
$1/4$ cup ($1/2$ stick) butter, softened
1 egg
2 tablespoons milk

1. Preheat oven to 350°. Empty contents of jar into large mixing bowl. Add honey, butter or margarine, egg and milk.
2. Beat on low speed or by hand until dough is completely mixed.
3. Roll pieces of dough into 1-inch balls and place 3 inches apart on lightly greased cookie sheet.
4. Bake for 10 to 12 minutes or until cookies are golden brown. Remove from oven and let cookies cool on cookie sheet for 1 minute, then transfer to cooling rack. (Makes $3^1/2$ to 4 dozen.)

www.cookbookresources.com

Thank You

Holiday Honey-Spice Cookies

$1/2$ cup honey
$1/4$ cup ($1/2$ stick) butter, softened
1 egg
2 tablespoons milk

1. Preheat oven to 350°. Empty contents of jar into large mixing bowl. Add honey, butter or margarine, egg and milk.
2. Beat on low speed or by hand until dough is completely mixed.
3. Roll pieces of dough into 1-inch balls and place 3 inches apart on lightly greased cookie sheet.
4. Bake for 10 to 12 minutes or until cookies are golden brown. Remove from oven and let cookies cool on cookie sheet for 1 minute, then transfer to cooling rack. (Makes $3^1/2$ to 4 dozen.)

Holiday Honey-Spice Cookies

$1/2$ cup honey
$1/4$ cup ($1/2$ stick) butter, softened
1 egg
2 tablespoons milk

1. Preheat oven to 350°. Empty contents of jar into large mixing bowl. Add honey, butter or margarine, egg and milk.
2. Beat on low speed or by hand until dough is completely mixed.
3. Roll pieces of dough into 1-inch balls and place 3 inches apart on lightly greased cookie sheet.
4. Bake for 10 to 12 minutes or until cookies are golden brown. Remove from oven and let cookies cool on cookie sheet for 1 minute, then transfer to cooling rack. (Makes $3^1/2$ to 4 dozen.)

Holiday Honey-Spice Cookies

$1/2$ cup honey
$1/4$ cup ($1/2$ stick) butter, softened
1 egg
2 tablespoons milk

1. Preheat oven to 350°. Empty contents of jar into large mixing bowl. Add honey, butter or margarine, egg and milk.
2. Beat on low speed or by hand until dough is completely mixed.
3. Roll pieces of dough into 1-inch balls and place 3 inches apart on lightly greased cookie sheet.
4. Bake for 10 to 12 minutes or until cookies are golden brown. Remove from oven and let cookies cool on cookie sheet for 1 minute, then transfer to cooling rack. (Makes $3^1/2$ to 4 dozen.)

Happy Birthday

Happy Holidays

Merry Christmas

Colorful Candy Cookies

Colorful Candy Cookies

Candy cookies are really sugar cookies speckled with colorful, candy-coated chocolate.

Ingredients for jar:
1 cup sugar
$1/2$ cup packed light brown sugar
2 cups flour
1 teaspoon baking soda
$1/4$ teaspoon salt
1 cup M&M candies

Instructions for jar:
1. Place sugar in 1-quart jar and smooth over top to make even.
2. Spoon brown sugar over and pack down evenly.
3. In small bowl, combine flour, baking soda and salt. Stir to mix. Spoon over brown sugar in jar, pressing down evenly.
4. Pour candies over flour mixture and place lid on jar.

Colorful Candy Cookies
Instructions for baking:

$^3/_4$ cup (1$^1/_2$ sticks) butter, softened
2 eggs

1. Preheat oven to 350°. Empty contents of jar into large bowl.

2. Add butter or margarine and eggs.

3. Beat by hand, so you don't break candies, until dough is thoroughly mixed.

4. Drop by rounded teaspoonfuls onto ungreased cookie sheet. Bake for 10 to 12 minutes until edges are browned.

5. Remove from oven and let cookies cool on cookie sheet for 1 minute, then transfer to cooling rack. (Makes 3 to 3$^1/_2$ dozen.)

"*M*ake new friends, both young and old, one in Silver, the other Gold."

Colorful Candy Cookies

³/₄ cup (1¹/₂ sticks) butter, softened
2 eggs

1. Preheat oven to 350°. Empty contents of jar into large bowl.
2. Add butter or margarine and eggs.
3. Beat by hand, so you don't break candies, until dough is thoroughly mixed.
4. Drop by rounded teaspoonfuls onto ungreased cookie sheet. Bake for 10 to 12 minutes until edges are browned.
5. Remove from oven and let cookies cool on cookie sheet for 1 minute, then transfer to cooling rack. (Makes 3 to 3¹/₂ dozen.)

Colorful Candy Cookies

³/₄ cup (1¹/₂ sticks) butter, softened
2 eggs

1. Preheat oven to 350°. Empty contents of jar into large bowl.
2. Add butter or margarine and eggs.
3. Beat by hand, so you don't break candies, until dough is thoroughly mixed.
4. Drop by rounded teaspoonfuls onto ungreased cookie sheet. Bake for 10 to 12 minutes until edges are browned.
5. Remove from oven and let cookies cool on cookie sheet for 1 minute, then transfer to cooling rack. (Makes 3 to 3¹/₂ dozen.)

Colorful Candy Cookies

³/₄ cup (1¹/₂ sticks) butter, softened
2 eggs .

1. Preheat oven to 350°. Empty contents of jar into large bowl.
2. Add butter or margarine and eggs.
3. Beat by hand, so you don't break candies, until dough is thoroughly mixed.
4. Drop by rounded teaspoonfuls onto ungreased cookie sheet. Bake for 10 to 12 minutes until edges are browned.
5. Remove from oven and let cookies cool on cookie sheet for 1 minute, then transfer to cooling rack. (Makes 3 to 3¹/₂ dozen.)

You're the Best

For My Good Friend

Colorful Candy Cookies

³/₄ cup (1¹/₂ sticks) butter, softened
2 eggs

1. Preheat oven to 350°. Empty contents of jar into large bowl.
2. Add butter or margarine and eggs.
3. Beat by hand, so you don't break candies, until dough is thoroughly mixed.
4. Drop by rounded teaspoonfuls onto ungreased cookie sheet. Bake for 10 to 12 minutes until edges are browned.
5. Remove from oven and let cookies cool on cookie sheet for 1 minute, then transfer to cooling rack. (Makes 3 to 3¹/₂ dozen.)

www.cookbookresources.com

Colorful Candy Cookies

³/₄ cup (1¹/₂ sticks) butter, softened
2 eggs

1. Preheat oven to 350°. Empty contents of jar into large bowl.
2. Add butter or margarine and eggs.
3. Beat by hand, so you don't break candies, until dough is thoroughly mixed.
4. Drop by rounded teaspoonfuls onto ungreased cookie sheet. Bake for 10 to 12 minutes until edges are browned.
5. Remove from oven and let cookies cool on cookie sheet for 1 minute, then transfer to cooling rack. (Makes 3 to 3¹/₂ dozen.)

www.cookbookresources.com

Colorful Candy Cookies

³/₄ cup (1¹/₂ sticks) butter, softened
2 eggs

1. Preheat oven to 350°. Empty contents of jar into large bowl.
2. Add butter or margarine and eggs.
3. Beat by hand, so you don't break candies, until dough is thoroughly mixed.
4. Drop by rounded teaspoonfuls onto ungreased cookie sheet. Bake for 10 to 12 minutes until edges are browned.
5. Remove from oven and let cookies cool on cookie sheet for 1 minute, then transfer to cooling rack. (Makes 3 to 3¹/₂ dozen.)

www.cookbookresources.com

Happy Birthday

Happy Holidays

Merry Christmas

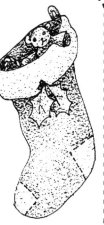

Malted Milk Crunchies

Malted Milk Crunchies

These crunchy cookies have the flavor
of malted milk balls.

Ingredients for jar:
$^1/_2$ cup sugar
$1^1/_4$ cups malted milk powder
2 cups flour
$^1/_2$ teaspoon baking powder
$^1/_4$ teaspoon salt
$^3/_4$ cup miniature-chocolate chips

Instructions for jar:
1. Pour sugar into 1-quart jar and smooth over to even out.
2. Spoon malted milk powder over sugar and even out. Press down lightly.
3. Spoon flour on top of malted milk powder. Press down lightly and even out.
4. Pour baking powder and salt over flour.
5. Add chocolate chips on top of flour and press down firmly to fit into jar. Place lid on jar.

Malted Milk Crunchies

Instructions for baking:

$^3/_4$ cup (1$^1/_2$ sticks) butter, softened
2 eggs

1. Preheat oven to 350°. Empty contents of jar into large bowl.

2. Add butter or margarine and eggs.

3. Beat on low speed or by hand until dough is thoroughly mixed. Drop by rounded teaspoonfuls onto ungreased cookie sheet and bake for 10 minutes or until edges are lightly browned.

4. Remove from oven and let cookies cool on cookie sheet for 1 minute, then transfer to cooling rack. (Makes 3 to 3$^1/_2$ dozen.)

"Grief can take care of itself, but to get the full value of joy you must have somebody to divide it with."

Mark Twain

Malted Milk Crunchies

$^3/_4$ cup ($1^1/_2$ sticks) butter, softened
2 eggs

1. Preheat oven to 350°. Empty contents of jar into large bowl.
2. Add butter or margarine and eggs.
3. Beat on low speed or by hand until dough is thoroughly mixed. Drop by rounded teaspoonfuls onto ungreased cookie sheet and bake for 10 minutes or until edges are lightly browned.
4. Remove from oven and let cookies cool on cookie sheet for 1 minute, then transfer to cooling rack. (Makes 3 to $3^1/_2$ dozen.)

www.cookbookresources.com

Malted Milk Crunchies

$^3/_4$ cup ($1^1/_2$ sticks) butter, softened
2 eggs

1. Preheat oven to 350°. Empty contents of jar into large bowl.
2. Add butter or margarine and eggs.
3. Beat on low speed or by hand until dough is thoroughly mixed. Drop by rounded teaspoonfuls onto ungreased cookie sheet and bake for 10 minutes or until edges are lightly browned.
4. Remove from oven and let cookies cool on cookie sheet for 1 minute, then transfer to cooling rack. (Makes 3 to $3^1/_2$ dozen.)

www.cookbookresources.com

Malted Milk Crunchies

$^3/_4$ cup ($1^1/_2$ sticks) butter, softened
2 eggs

1. Preheat oven to 350°. Empty contents of jar into large bowl.
2. Add butter or margarine and eggs.
3. Beat on low speed or by hand until dough is thoroughly mixed. Drop by rounded teaspoonfuls onto ungreased cookie sheet and bake for 10 minutes or until edges are lightly browned.
4. Remove from oven and let cookies cool on cookie sheet for 1 minute, then transfer to cooling rack. (Makes 3 to $3^1/_2$ dozen.)

www.cookbookresources.com

You're a Doll

Malted Milk Crunchies

$^3/_4$ cup ($1^1/_2$ sticks) butter, softened
2 eggs

1. Preheat oven to 350°. Empty contents of jar into large bowl.
2. Add butter or margarine and eggs.
3. Beat on low speed or by hand until dough is thoroughly mixed. Drop by rounded teaspoonfuls onto ungreased cookie sheet and bake for 10 minutes or until edges are lightly browned.
4. Remove from oven and let cookies cool on cookie sheet for 1 minute, then transfer to cooling rack. (Makes 3 to $3^1/_2$ dozen.)

www.cookbookresources.com

Malted Milk Crunchies

$^3/_4$ cup ($1^1/_2$ sticks) butter, softened
2 eggs

1. Preheat oven to 350°. Empty contents of jar into large bowl.
2. Add butter or margarine and eggs.
3. Beat on low speed or by hand until dough is thoroughly mixed. Drop by rounded teaspoonfuls onto ungreased cookie sheet and bake for 10 minutes or until edges are lightly browned.
4. Remove from oven and let cookies cool on cookie sheet for 1 minute, then transfer to cooling rack. (Makes 3 to $3^1/_2$ dozen.)

www.cookbookresources.com

Malted Milk Crunchies

$^3/_4$ cup ($1^1/_2$ sticks) butter, softened
2 eggs

1. Preheat oven to 350°. Empty contents of jar into large bowl.
2. Add butter or margarine and eggs.
3. Beat on low speed or by hand until dough is thoroughly mixed. Drop by rounded teaspoonfuls onto ungreased cookie sheet and bake for 10 minutes or until edges are lightly browned.
4. Remove from oven and let cookies cool on cookie sheet for 1 minute, then transfer to cooling rack. (Makes 3 to $3^1/_2$ dozen.)

www.cookbookresources.com

Happy Birthday

Happy Holidays

Merry Christmas

Butterscotch Snaps

Butterscotch Snaps

Nicely round, crunchy brown cookies have a hint of cinnamon and burst with sweet butterscotch chips.

Ingredients for jar:
1 cup packed light brown sugar
2 cups flour
1 teaspoon baking powder
$1/2$ teaspoon baking soda
$1/2$ teaspoon salt
1 teaspoon cinnamon
$1^{1}/_{4}$ cups butterscotch baking chips

Instructions for jar:
1. Add brown sugar to 1-quart jar and pack down firmly and evenly.
2. In medium bowl, combine flour, baking powder, baking soda and salt. Spoon half of flour into jar over brown sugar and even out.
3. Add cinnamon to remaining half of flour mixture and stir to mix. Spoon cinnamon-flour mixture over flour mixture in jar and press down firmly. (You don't have to divide the flour, but adding cinnamon to one half gives the ingredients a nice layered look in the jar.)
4. Sprinkle butterscotch chips over flour, pressing down to fit all of them in the jar. Place lid on jar and close.

Butterscotch Snaps

Instructions for baking:

2 eggs
$^2/_3$ cup salad oil
1 teaspoon vanilla

1. Preheat oven to 400°. Empty contents of jar into large bowl. Add eggs, oil and vanilla.

2. Beat on low speed or by hand until dough is thoroughly mixed.

3. Roll heaping teaspoonfuls of dough into balls and place 3 inches apart on ungreased cookie sheet. Bake for 7 minutes.

4. Remove from oven and let cookies cool on cookie sheet for 1 minute, then transfer to cooling rack. (Makes $3^1/_2$ to 4 dozen.)

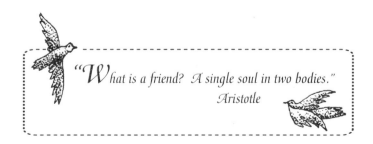

"What is a friend? A single soul in two bodies."
Aristotle

Butterscotch Snaps

2 eggs
$2/3$ cup salad oil
1 teaspoon vanilla

1. Preheat oven to 400°. Empty contents of jar into large bowl. Add eggs, oil and vanilla.
2. Beat on low speed or by hand until dough is thoroughly mixed.
3. Roll heaping teaspoonfuls of dough into balls and place 3 inches apart on ungreased cookie sheet. Bake for 7 minutes.
4. Remove from oven and let cookies cool on cookie sheet for 1 minute, then transfer to cooling rack. (Makes $3^1/2$ to 4 dozen.)

www.cookbookresources.com

Butterscotch Snaps

2 eggs
$2/3$ cup salad oil
1 teaspoon vanilla

1. Preheat oven to 400°. Empty contents of jar into large bowl. Add eggs, oil and vanilla.
2. Beat on low speed or by hand until dough is thoroughly mixed.
3. Roll heaping teaspoonfuls of dough into balls and place 3 inches apart on ungreased cookie sheet. Bake for 7 minutes.
4. Remove from oven and let cookies cool on cookie sheet for 1 minute, then transfer to cooling rack. (Makes $3^1/2$ to 4 dozen.)

www.cookbookresources.com

Butterscotch Snaps

2 eggs
$2/3$ cup salad oil
1 teaspoon vanilla

1. Preheat oven to 400°. Empty contents of jar into large bowl. Add eggs, oil and vanilla.
2. Beat on low speed or by hand until dough is thoroughly mixed.
3. Roll heaping teaspoonfuls of dough into balls and place 3 inches apart on ungreased cookie sheet. Bake for 7 minutes.
4. Remove from oven and let cookies cool on cookie sheet for 1 minute, then transfer to cooling rack. (Makes $3^1/2$ to 4 dozen.)

www.cookbookresources.com

Thinking of You

Butterscotch Snaps

2 eggs
²/₃ cup salad oil
1 teaspoon vanilla

1. Preheat oven to 400°. Empty contents of jar into large bowl. Add eggs, oil and vanilla.
2. Beat on low speed or by hand until dough is thoroughly mixed.
3. Roll heaping teaspoonfuls of dough into balls and place 3 inches apart on ungreased cookie sheet. Bake for 7 minutes.
4. Remove from oven and let cookies cool on cookie sheet for 1 minute, then transfer to cooling rack. (Makes 3¹/₂ to 4 dozen.)

www.cookbookresources.com

Butterscotch Snaps

2 eggs
²/₃ cup salad oil
1 teaspoon vanilla

1. Preheat oven to 400°. Empty contents of jar into large bowl. Add eggs, oil and vanilla.
2. Beat on low speed or by hand until dough is thoroughly mixed.
3. Roll heaping teaspoonfuls of dough into balls and place 3 inches apart on ungreased cookie sheet. Bake for 7 minutes.
4. Remove from oven and let cookies cool on cookie sheet for 1 minute, then transfer to cooling rack. (Makes 3¹/₂ to 4 dozen.)

www.cookbookresources.com

Butterscotch Snaps

2 eggs
²/₃ cup salad oil
1 teaspoon vanilla

1. Preheat oven to 400°. Empty contents of jar into large bowl. Add eggs, oil and vanilla.
2. Beat on low speed or by hand until dough is thoroughly mixed.
3. Roll heaping teaspoonfuls of dough into balls and place 3 inches apart on ungreased cookie sheet. Bake for 7 minutes.
4. Remove from oven and let cookies cool on cookie sheet for 1 minute, then transfer to cooling rack. (Makes 3¹/₂ to 4 dozen.)

www.cookbookresources.com

Happy Birthday

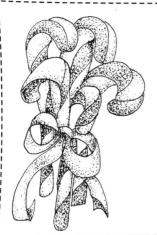

Happy Holidays

Merry Christmas!

Gingerbread Rounds

Gingerbread Rounds

Perfectly round, deep brown delicately flavored cookies have a crispy crunch.

Ingredients for jar:

$1^{1}/_{2}$ cups sugar
3 cups flour
$1^{1}/_{2}$ teaspoons baking soda
$1^{1}/_{2}$ teaspoons baking powder
$^{1}/_{2}$ teaspoon salt
$1^{1}/_{2}$ teaspoons cinnamon
3 teaspoons ground ginger

Instructions for jar:

1. In large bowl, combine all ingredients and mix well.
2. Spoon cookie mixture into 1-quart jar, packing down after each addition so all mixture fits.
3. Put lid on jar to close.

Gingerbread Rounds

Instructions for baking:

2 eggs
1 cup salad oil
$^1/_3$ cup molasses
Several tablespoons sugar

1. Preheat oven to 350°. Empty contents of jar into large bowl.

2. Add eggs, oil and molasses. Beat on low speed until dough is thoroughly mixed.

3. Roll teaspoonfuls of dough into balls and dip in sugar to coat. Place 3 inches apart on lightly greased cookie sheet.

4. Bake for 12 to 14 minutes. Remove from oven and let cookies cool on cookie sheet for 1 minute, then transfer to cooling rack. (Makes 4 dozen.)

"A good friend is hard to find, hard to lose, and impossible to forget…"

Anonymous

Gingerbread Rounds

2 eggs
1 cup salad oil
⅓ cup molasses
Several tablespoons sugar

1. Preheat oven to 350°. Empty contents of jar into large bowl.
2. Add eggs, oil and molasses. Beat on low speed until dough is thoroughly mixed.
3. Roll teaspoonfuls of dough into balls and dip in sugar to coat. Place 3 inches apart on lightly greased cookie sheet.
4. Bake for 12 to 14 minutes. Remove from oven and let cookies cool on cookie sheet for 1 minute, then transfer to cooling rack. (Makes 4 dozen.)

www.cookbookresources.com

Gingerbread Rounds

2 eggs
1 cup salad oil
⅓ cup molasses
Several tablespoons sugar

1. Preheat oven to 350°. Empty contents of jar into large bowl.
2. Add eggs, oil and molasses. Beat on low speed until dough is thoroughly mixed.
3. Roll teaspoonfuls of dough into balls and dip in sugar to coat. Place 3 inches apart on lightly greased cookie sheet.
4. Bake for 12 to 14 minutes. Remove from oven and let cookies cool on cookie sheet for 1 minute, then transfer to cooling rack. (Makes 4 dozen.)

www.cookbookresources.com

Gingerbread Rounds

2 eggs
1 cup salad oil
⅓ cup molasses
Several tablespoons sugar

1. Preheat oven to 350°. Empty contents of jar into large bowl.
2. Add eggs, oil and molasses. Beat on low speed until dough is thoroughly mixed.
3. Roll teaspoonfuls of dough into balls and dip in sugar to coat. Place 3 inches apart on lightly greased cookie sheet.
4. Bake for 12 to 14 minutes. Remove from oven and let cookies cool on cookie sheet for 1 minute, then transfer to cooling rack. (Makes 4 dozen.)

www.cookbookresources.com

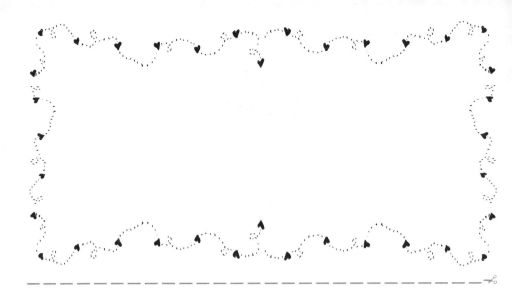

✂

✂

You're a Pal

Gingerbread Rounds

2 eggs
1 cup salad oil
$^1/_3$ cup molasses
Several tablespoons sugar

1. Preheat oven to 350°. Empty contents of jar into large bowl.
2. Add eggs, oil and molasses. Beat on low speed until dough is thoroughly mixed.
3. Roll teaspoonfuls of dough into balls and dip in sugar to coat. Place 3 inches apart on lightly greased cookie sheet.
4. Bake for 12 to 14 minutes. Remove from oven and let cookies cool on cookie sheet for 1 minute, then transfer to cooling rack. (Makes 4 dozen.)

www.cookbookresources.com

Gingerbread Rounds

2 eggs
1 cup salad oil
$^1/_3$ cup molasses
Several tablespoons sugar

1. Preheat oven to 350°. Empty contents of jar into large bowl.
2. Add eggs, oil and molasses. Beat on low speed until dough is thoroughly mixed.
3. Roll teaspoonfuls of dough into balls and dip in sugar to coat. Place 3 inches apart on lightly greased cookie sheet.
4. Bake for 12 to 14 minutes. Remove from oven and let cookies cool on cookie sheet for 1 minute, then transfer to cooling rack. (Makes 4 dozen.)

www.cookbookresources.com

Gingerbread Rounds

2 eggs
1 cup salad oil
$^1/_3$ cup molasses
Several tablespoons sugar

1. Preheat oven to 350°. Empty contents of jar into large bowl.
2. Add eggs, oil and molasses. Beat on low speed until dough is thoroughly mixed.
3. Roll teaspoonfuls of dough into balls and dip in sugar to coat. Place 3 inches apart on lightly greased cookie sheet.
4. Bake for 12 to 14 minutes. Remove from oven and let cookies cool on cookie sheet for 1 minute, then transfer to cooling rack. (Makes 4 dozen.)

www.cookbookresources.com

Happy
Birthday

- ✂

Happy Holidays

- ✂

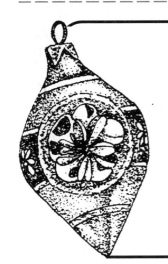

Merry Christmas

Choco-Cranberry Nuggets

Choco-Cranberry Nuggets

These wonderful little cookies combine the flavor of chocolate and fruit, similar to the classic cherries and chocolate combination. Crispy on the outside and soft on the inside, these little mound-shaped cookies are sure winners.

Ingredients for jar:

$2^1/_2$ cups flour
1 cup sugar
1 teaspoon baking powder
1 teaspoon salt
$^3/_4$ cup dried, sweetened cranberries
$^3/_4$ cup miniature-chocolate chips

Instructions for jar:

1. In medium bowl, combine flour, sugar, baking powder and salt. Stir well to mix.
2. Place half of flour mixture in 1-quart jar and press down firmly.
3. Place cranberries in jar over flour mixture and then sprinkle chocolate chips over cranberries. Press down firmly.
4. Spoon remaining half of flour mixture over chocolate chips. Place lid on jar to close.

Choco-Cranberry Nuggets

Instructions for baking:

1 teaspoon vanilla
2 eggs
³/₄ cup salad oil

1. Preheat oven to 375°. Empty contents of jar into large mixing bowl.

2. Add vanilla, eggs and oil.

3. Beat on low speed or by hand to mix until dough is thoroughly blended. (Dough will be slightly crumbly.)

4. Using your hands, shape into 1¹/₂-inch balls and roll in sugar. (Cookies will be irregularly shaped and that's ok.) Place 3 inches apart on ungreased cookie sheet.

5. Bake for 10 minutes or until very lightly browned around edges.

6. Remove from oven and let cookies cool on cookie sheet for 1 minute, then transfer to cooling rack. (Makes 3 dozen.)

"*I always knew looking back on the tears would make me laugh. But I never knew looking back on the laughs would make me cry.*"

Anonymous

Choco-Cranberry Nuggets

1 teaspoon vanilla
2 eggs
$3/4$ cup salad oil

1. Preheat oven to 375°. Empty contents of jar into large mixing bowl.
2. Add vanilla, eggs and oil.
3. Beat on low speed or by hand to mix until dough is thoroughly blended. (Dough will be slightly crumbly.)
4. Using your hands, shape into $1^1/_2$-inch balls and roll in sugar. (Cookies will be irregularly shaped and that's ok.) Place 3 inches apart on ungreased cookie sheet.
5. Bake for 10 minutes or until very lightly browned around edges.
6. Remove from oven and let cookies cool on cookie sheet for 1 minute, then transfer to cooling rack. (Makes 3 dozen.)

www.cookbookresources.com

Choco-Cranberry Nuggets

1 teaspoon vanilla
2 eggs
$3/4$ cup salad oil

1. Preheat oven to 375°. Empty contents of jar into large mixing bowl.
2. Add vanilla, eggs and oil.
3. Beat on low speed or by hand to mix until dough is thoroughly blended. (Dough will be slightly crumbly.)
4. Using your hands, shape into $1^1/_2$-inch balls and roll in sugar. (Cookies will be irregularly shaped and that's ok.) Place 3 inches apart on ungreased cookie sheet.
5. Bake for 10 minutes or until very lightly browned around edges.
6. Remove from oven and let cookies cool on cookie sheet for 1 minute, then transfer to cooling rack. (Makes 3 dozen.)

www.cookbookresources.com

Choco-Cranberry Nuggets

1 teaspoon vanilla
2 eggs
$3/4$ cup salad oil

1. Preheat oven to 375°. Empty contents of jar into large mixing bowl.
2. Add vanilla, eggs and oil.
3. Beat on low speed or by hand to mix until dough is thoroughly blended. (Dough will be slightly crumbly.)
4. Using your hands, shape into $1^1/_2$-inch balls and roll in sugar. (Cookies will be irregularly shaped and that's ok.) Place 3 inches apart on ungreased cookie sheet.
5. Bake for 10 minutes or until very lightly browned around edges.
6. Remove from oven and let cookies cool on cookie sheet for 1 minute, then transfer to cooling rack. (Makes 3 dozen.)

www.cookbookresources.com

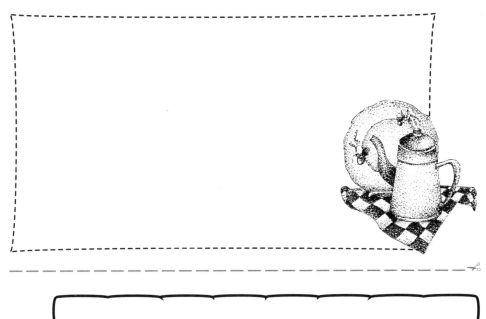

Best Wishes

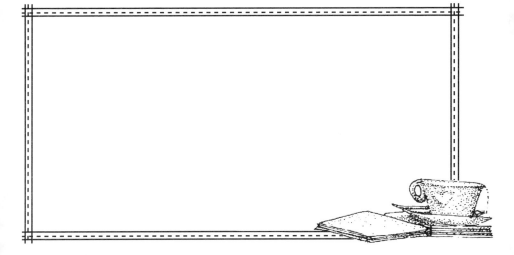

Choco-Cranberry Nuggets

1 teaspoon vanilla
2 eggs
$^3/_4$ cup salad oil

1. Preheat oven to 375°. Empty contents of jar into large mixing bowl.
2. Add vanilla, eggs and oil.
3. Beat on low speed or by hand to mix until dough is thoroughly blended. (Dough will be slightly crumbly.)
4. Using your hands, shape into $1^1/_2$-inch balls and roll in sugar. (Cookies will be irregularly shaped and that's ok.) Place 3 inches apart on ungreased cookie sheet.
5. Bake for 10 minutes or until very lightly browned around edges.
6. Remove from oven and let cookies cool on cookie sheet for 1 minute, then transfer to cooling rack. (Makes 3 dozen.)

www.cookbookresources.com

Choco-Cranberry Nuggets

1 teaspoon vanilla
2 eggs
$^3/_4$ cup salad oil

1. Preheat oven to 375°. Empty contents of jar into large mixing bowl.
2. Add vanilla, eggs and oil.
3. Beat on low speed or by hand to mix until dough is thoroughly blended. (Dough will be slightly crumbly.)
4. Using your hands, shape into $1^1/_2$-inch balls and roll in sugar. (Cookies will be irregularly shaped and that's ok.) Place 3 inches apart on ungreased cookie sheet.
5. Bake for 10 minutes or until very lightly browned around edges.
6. Remove from oven and let cookies cool on cookie sheet for 1 minute, then transfer to cooling rack. (Makes 3 dozen.)

www.cookbookresources.com

Choco-Cranberry Nuggets

1 teaspoon vanilla
2 eggs
$^3/_4$ cup salad oil

1. Preheat oven to 375°. Empty contents of jar into large mixing bowl.
2. Add vanilla, eggs and oil.
3. Beat on low speed or by hand to mix until dough is thoroughly blended. (Dough will be slightly crumbly.)
4. Using your hands, shape into $1^1/_2$-inch balls and roll in sugar. (Cookies will be irregularly shaped and that's ok.) Place 3 inches apart on ungreased cookie sheet.
5. Bake for 10 minutes or until very lightly browned around edges.
6. Remove from oven and let cookies cool on cookie sheet for 1 minute, then transfer to cooling rack. (Makes 3 dozen.)

www.cookbookresources.com

Happy Birthday

Happy Holidays

Merry Christmas

White Chocolate-Macadamia Nut Rounds

White Chocolate Macadamia Nut Rounds

These thin crispy cookies are loaded with macadamia nuts and white chocolate.

Ingredients for jar:

$^1/_2$ cup packed light brown sugar
$^1/_4$ cup sugar
$1^1/_4$ cups flour
$^1/_2$ teaspoon baking soda
$^1/_8$ teaspoon salt
1 tablespoon dried, ground orange peel*, optional
1 cup white chocolate chips
1 cup coarsely chopped, toasted macadamia nuts**

Instructions for jar:

1. Place brown sugar in 1-quart jar and pack down evenly.
2. Pour sugar on top and smooth over.
3. In medium bowl, combine flour, baking soda, salt and orange peel. Stir well to mix. Spoon flour mixture over sugar carefully in several additions, pressing down firmly after each addition.
4. Place white chocolate chips over flour mixture and press down firmly.
5. Add macadamia nuts over chips. Press down firmly to fit them all and place lid on jar.

*Dried, ground orange peel can be found in the spice section of your grocery store.
**To toast macadamia nuts, spread them out in a single layer on a cookie sheet. Bake at 250° for about 5 minutes or until they are lightly brown. Be careful not to let them burn.

White Chocolate-
Macadamia Nut Rounds

Instructions for baking:

$^1/_2$ cup (1 stick) butter, softened
1 egg

1. Preheat oven to 350°. Empty contents of jar into large bowl.

2. Add butter or margarine and egg.

3. Beat on low speed or by hand until well mixed.

4. Drop by rounded teaspoonfuls onto ungreased cookie sheet. Bake for 10 to 12 minutes.

5. Remove from oven and let cookies cool on cookie sheet for 1 minute, then transfer to cooling rack. (Makes $2^1/_2$ to 3 dozen.)

"*A* good friend remembers what we were and sees what we can be."

Anonymous

White Chocolate-Macadamia Nut Rounds

$^1/_2$ cup (1 stick) butter, softened
1 egg

1. Preheat oven to 350°. Empty contents of jar into large bowl.
2. Add butter or margarine and egg.
3. Beat on low speed or by hand until well mixed.
4. Drop by rounded teaspoonfuls onto ungreased cookie sheet. Bake for 10 to 12 minutes.
5. Remove from oven and let cookies cool on cookie sheet for 1 minute, then transfer to cooling rack. (Makes $2^1/_2$ to 3 dozen.)

www.cookbookresources.com

White Chocolate-Macadamia Nut Rounds

$^1/_2$ cup (1 stick) butter, softened
1 egg

1. Preheat oven to 350°. Empty contents of jar into large bowl.
2. Add butter or margarine and egg.
3. Beat on low speed or by hand until well mixed.
4. Drop by rounded teaspoonfuls onto ungreased cookie sheet. Bake for 10 to 12 minutes.
5. Remove from oven and let cookies cool on cookie sheet for 1 minute, then transfer to cooling rack. (Makes $2^1/_2$ to 3 dozen.)

www.cookbookresources.com

White Chocolate-Macadamia Nut Rounds

$^1/_2$ cup (1 stick) butter, softened
1 egg

1. Preheat oven to 350°. Empty contents of jar into large bowl.
2. Add butter or margarine and egg.
3. Beat on low speed or by hand until well mixed.
4. Drop by rounded teaspoonfuls onto ungreased cookie sheet. Bake for 10 to 12 minutes.
5. Remove from oven and let cookies cool on cookie sheet for 1 minute, then transfer to cooling rack. (Makes $2^1/_2$ to 3 dozen.)

www.cookbookresources.com

Just Because

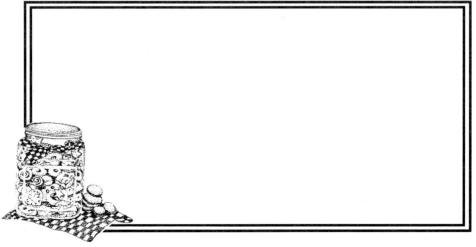

White Chocolate-Macadamia Nut Rounds

¹/₂ cup (1 stick) butter, softened
1 egg

1. Preheat oven to 350°. Empty contents of jar into large bowl.
2. Add butter or margarine and egg.
3. Beat on low speed or by hand until well mixed.
4. Drop by rounded teaspoonfuls onto ungreased cookie sheet. Bake for 10 to 12 minutes.
5. Remove from oven and let cookies cool on cookie sheet for 1 minute, then transfer to cooling rack. (Makes 2$\frac{1}{2}$ to 3 dozen.)

White Chocolate-Macadamia Nut Rounds

¹/₂ cup (1 stick) butter, softened
1 egg

1. Preheat oven to 350°. Empty contents of jar into large bowl.
2. Add butter or margarine and egg.
3. Beat on low speed or by hand until well mixed.
4. Drop by rounded teaspoonfuls onto ungreased cookie sheet. Bake for 10 to 12 minutes.
5. Remove from oven and let cookies cool on cookie sheet for 1 minute, then transfer to cooling rack. (Makes 2$\frac{1}{2}$ to 3 dozen.)

White Chocolate-Macadamia Nut Rounds

¹/₂ cup (1 stick) butter, softened
1 egg

1. Preheat oven to 350°. Empty contents of jar into large bowl.
2. Add butter or margarine and egg.
3. Beat on low speed or by hand until well mixed.
4. Drop by rounded teaspoonfuls onto ungreased cookie sheet. Bake for 10 to 12 minutes.
5. Remove from oven and let cookies cool on cookie sheet for 1 minute, then transfer to cooling rack. (Makes 2$\frac{1}{2}$ to 3 dozen.)

Happy Birthday

Happy Holidays

Merry Christmas

Walnut-Cinnamon Balls

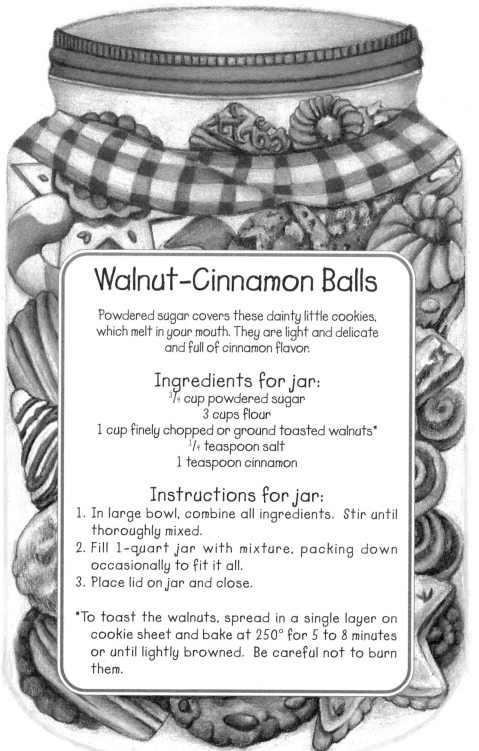

Walnut-Cinnamon Balls

Powdered sugar covers these dainty little cookies, which melt in your mouth. They are light and delicate and full of cinnamon flavor.

Ingredients for jar:
$^3/_4$ cup powdered sugar
3 cups flour
1 cup finely chopped or ground toasted walnuts*
$^1/_4$ teaspoon salt
1 teaspoon cinnamon

Instructions for jar:
1. In large bowl, combine all ingredients. Stir until thoroughly mixed.
2. Fill 1-quart jar with mixture, packing down occasionally to fit it all.
3. Place lid on jar and close.

*To toast the walnuts, spread in a single layer on cookie sheet and bake at 250° for 5 to 8 minutes or until lightly browned. Be careful not to burn them.

Walnut-Cinnamon Balls

Instructions for baking:

1¹/₂ cups (3 sticks) butter, softened
1 teaspoon vanilla
¹/₂ cup powdered sugar

1. Preheat oven to 325°. Place butter or margarine and vanilla in large bowl. Beat on low speed and add contents of jar a little at a time, beating well after each addition.

2. Roll dough into balls 1-inch wide and place 2 inches apart on ungreased cookie sheet. Bake for 13 to 15 minutes.

3. Remove from oven and let cookies cool on cookie sheet for 1 minute, then transfer to cooling rack. Let cool for 10 minutes and then roll in powdered sugar (about ¹/₂ cup) to coat . (Makes 4 dozen.)

"*Love is blind, but friendship closes its eyes.*"
Anonymous

Walnut-Cinnamon Balls

$1^1/_2$ cups (3 sticks) butter, softened
1 teaspoon vanilla
$^1/_2$ cup powdered sugar

1. Preheat oven to 325°. Place butter or margarine and vanilla in large bowl. Beat on low speed and add contents of jar a little at a time, beating well after each addition.
2. Roll dough into balls 1-inch wide and place 2 inches apart on ungreased cookie sheet. Bake for 13 to 15 minutes.
3. Remove from oven and let cookies cool on cookie sheet for 1 minute, then transfer to cooling rack. Let cool for 10 minutes and then roll in powdered sugar (about $^1/_2$ cup) to coat . (Makes 4 dozen.)

Walnut-Cinnamon Balls

$1^1/_2$ cups (3 sticks) butter, softened
1 teaspoon vanilla
$^1/_2$ cup powdered sugar

1. Preheat oven to 325°. Place butter or margarine and vanilla in large bowl. Beat on low speed and add contents of jar a little at a time, beating well after each addition.
2. Roll dough into balls 1-inch wide and place 2 inches apart on ungreased cookie sheet. Bake for 13 to 15 minutes.
3. Remove from oven and let cookies cool on cookie sheet for 1 minute, then transfer to cooling rack. Let cool for 10 minutes and then roll in powdered sugar (about $^1/_2$ cup) to coat . (Makes 4 dozen.)

www.cookbookresources.com

Walnut-Cinnamon Balls

$1^1/_2$ cups (3 sticks) butter, softened
1 teaspoon vanilla
$^1/_2$ cup powdered sugar

1. Preheat oven to 325°. Place butter or margarine and vanilla in large bowl. Beat on low speed and add contents of jar a little at a time, beating well after each addition.
2. Roll dough into balls 1-inch wide and place 2 inches apart on ungreased cookie sheet. Bake for 13 to 15 minutes.
3. Remove from oven and let cookies cool on cookie sheet for 1 minute, then transfer to cooling rack. Let cool for 10 minutes and then roll in powdered sugar (about $^1/_2$ cup) to coat . (Makes 4 dozen.)

www.cookbookresources.com

Thank You

Walnut-Cinnamon Balls

$1\frac{1}{2}$ cups (3 sticks) butter, softened
1 teaspoon vanilla
$\frac{1}{2}$ cup powdered sugar

1. Preheat oven to 325°. Place butter or margarine and vanilla in large bowl. Beat on low speed and add contents of jar a little at a time, beating well after each addition.
2. Roll dough into balls 1-inch wide and place 2 inches apart on ungreased cookie sheet. Bake for 13 to 15 minutes.
3. Remove from oven and let cookies cool on cookie sheet for 1 minute, then transfer to cooling rack. Let cool for 10 minutes and then roll in powdered sugar (about $\frac{1}{2}$ cup) to coat . (Makes 4 dozen.)

www.cookbookresources.com

Walnut-Cinnamon Balls

$1\frac{1}{2}$ cups (3 sticks) butter, softened
1 teaspoon vanilla
$\frac{1}{2}$ cup powdered sugar

1. Preheat oven to 325°. Place butter or margarine and vanilla in large bowl. Beat on low speed and add contents of jar a little at a time, beating well after each addition.
2. Roll dough into balls 1-inch wide and place 2 inches apart on ungreased cookie sheet. Bake for 13 to 15 minutes.
3. Remove from oven and let cookies cool on cookie sheet for 1 minute, then transfer to cooling rack. Let cool for 10 minutes and then roll in powdered sugar (about $\frac{1}{2}$ cup) to coat . (Makes 4 dozen.)

www.cookbookresources.com

Walnut-Cinnamon Balls

$1\frac{1}{2}$ cups (3 sticks) butter, softened
1 teaspoon vanilla
$\frac{1}{2}$ cup powdered sugar

1. Preheat oven to 325°. Place butter or margarine and vanilla in large bowl. Beat on low speed and add contents of jar a little at a time, beating well after each addition.
2. Roll dough into balls 1-inch wide and place 2 inches apart on ungreased cookie sheet. Bake for 13 to 15 minutes.
3. Remove from oven and let cookies cool on cookie sheet for 1 minute, then transfer to cooling rack. Let cool for 10 minutes and then roll in powdered sugar (about $\frac{1}{2}$ cup) to coat . (Makes 4 dozen.)

www.cookbookresources.com

Happy Birthday

Happy Holidays

Merry Christmas

Toffee-Chocolate Chippers

Toffee-Chocolate Chippers

This is a traditional chocolate chip cookie with a twist--bits of toffee scattered throughout. The cookie looks especially nice in the jar with all of its contrasting layers.

Ingredients for jar:
$1/4$ cup sugar
$1/2$ cup packed light brown sugar
$1^1/4$ cups flour
$1/4$ teaspoon baking soda
1 cup coarsely chopped walnuts
1 cup semi-sweet chocolate chips
$1/2$ cup almond toffee bits or crushed Heath bars

Instructions for jar:
1. Pour sugar in bottom of 1-quart jar and smooth over top.
2. Place brown sugar on top of sugar and pack down firmly and evenly.
3. Spoon flour over brown sugar and pack down. Pour baking soda over flour.
4. Sprinkle walnuts over flour and press down.
5. Place chocolate chips on walnuts and then sprinkle toffee bits over chocolate. Press down to fit.
6. Place lid on jar and close.

Toffee-Chocolate Chippers
Instructions for baking:

1 egg
1/2 cup (1 stick) butter, softened

1. Preheat oven to 375°. Empty contents of jar into large mixing bowl. Add egg and butter or margarine.

2. Beat on low speed or by hand to blend.

3. Once dough is thoroughly mixed, drop by rounded teaspoonfuls onto ungreased cookie sheet.

4. Bake for 8 to 10 minutes or until edges are brown. Remove from oven and let cookies cool on cookie sheet for 1 minute, then transfer to cooling rack. (Makes 3 dozen.)

> *"Friends are the chocolate chips in the cookie of life."*
> *Anonymous*

Toffee-Chocolate Chippers

1 egg
$1/2$ cup (1 stick) butter, softened

1. Preheat oven to 375°. Empty contents of jar into large mixing bowl. Add egg and butter or margarine.
2. Beat on low speed or by hand to blend.
3. Once dough is thoroughly mixed, drop by rounded teaspoonfuls onto ungreased cookie sheet.
4. Bake for 8 to 10 minutes or until edges are brown. Remove from oven and let cookies cool on cookie sheet for 1 minute, then transfer to cooling rack. (Makes 3 dozen.)

www.cookbookresources.com

Toffee-Chocolate Chippers

1 egg
$1/2$ cup (1 stick) butter, softened

1. Preheat oven to 375°. Empty contents of jar into large mixing bowl. Add egg and butter or margarine.
2. Beat on low speed or by hand to blend.
3. Once dough is thoroughly mixed, drop by rounded teaspoonfuls onto ungreased cookie sheet.
4. Bake for 8 to 10 minutes or until edges are brown. Remove from oven and let cookies cool on cookie sheet for 1 minute, then transfer to cooling rack. (Makes 3 dozen.)

www.cookbookresources.com

Toffee-Chocolate Chippers

1 egg
$1/2$ cup (1 stick) butter, softened

1. Preheat oven to 375°. Empty contents of jar into large mixing bowl. Add egg and butter or margarine.
2. Beat on low speed or by hand to blend.
3. Once dough is thoroughly mixed, drop by rounded teaspoonfuls onto ungreased cookie sheet.
4. Bake for 8 to 10 minutes or until edges are brown. Remove from oven and let cookies cool on cookie sheet for 1 minute, then transfer to cooling rack. (Makes 3 dozen.)

www.cookbookresources.com

You're the Best

For My Good Friend

Toffee-Chocolate Chippers

1 egg
$^1/_2$ cup (1 stick) butter, softened

1. Preheat oven to 375°. Empty contents of jar into large mixing bowl. Add egg and butter or margarine.
2. Beat on low speed or by hand to blend.
3. Once dough is thoroughly mixed, drop by rounded teaspoonfuls onto ungreased cookie sheet.
4. Bake for 8 to 10 minutes or until edges are brown. Remove from oven and let cookies cool on cookie sheet for 1 minute, then transfer to cooling rack. (Makes 3 dozen.)

www.cookbookresources.com

Toffee-Chocolate Chippers

1 egg
$^1/_2$ cup (1 stick) butter, softened

1. Preheat oven to 375°. Empty contents of jar into large mixing bowl. Add egg and butter or margarine.
2. Beat on low speed or by hand to blend.
3. Once dough is thoroughly mixed, drop by rounded teaspoonfuls onto ungreased cookie sheet.
4. Bake for 8 to 10 minutes or until edges are brown. Remove from oven and let cookies cool on cookie sheet for 1 minute, then transfer to cooling rack. (Makes 3 dozen.)

www.cookbookresources.com

Toffee-Chocolate Chippers

1 egg
$^1/_2$ cup (1 stick) butter, softened

1. Preheat oven to 375°. Empty contents of jar into large mixing bowl. Add egg and butter or margarine.
2. Beat on low speed or by hand to blend.
3. Once dough is thoroughly mixed, drop by rounded teaspoonfuls onto ungreased cookie sheet.
4. Bake for 8 to 10 minutes or until edges are brown. Remove from oven and let cookies cool on cookie sheet for 1 minute, then transfer to cooling rack. (Makes 3 dozen.)

www.cookbookresources.com

Happy Birthday

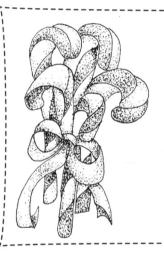

Happy Holidays

Merry Christmas!

Deluxe Oatmeal Cookies

Deluxe Oatmeal Cookies

Oatmeal cookies chock full of sweet cranberries, crunchy walnuts and tasty dates will entice everyone's taste buds.

Ingredients for jar:
$1/3$ cup sugar
$1/3$ cup packed light brown sugar
$1/2$ cup flour
$1/2$ teaspoon baking soda
1 cup quick-cooking oats
$1/2$ cup dried, sweetened cranberries
1 cup coarsely chopped walnuts
$1/2$ cup chopped dates

Instructions for jar:
1. Pour sugar into 1-quart jar and smooth over.
2. Spoon brown sugar over sugar and pack down firmly but evenly.
3. Spoon flour and baking soda over brown sugar and press down.
4. Pour in oats, then place cranberries on oats.
5. Place walnuts over cranberries and press down.
6. Add dates over walnuts and place lid on jar to close.

133

Deluxe Oatmeal Cookies
Instructions for baking:

$^1/_3$ cup ($5^1/_3$ tablespoons) butter, softened
1 egg
$^1/_2$ teaspoon vanilla

1. Preheat oven to 350°. Empty contents of jar into large mixing bowl.

2. Add butter or margarine, egg and vanilla.

3. Beat on low speed until dough is thoroughly blended.

4. Roll heaping teaspoonfuls of dough into balls and place 3 inches apart on ungreased cookie sheet.

5. Bake for 12 to 14 minutes or until edges are lightly browned. Remove from oven and let cookies cool on cookie sheet for 1 minute before transferring to cooling rack. (Makes 3 to $3^1/_2$ dozen.)

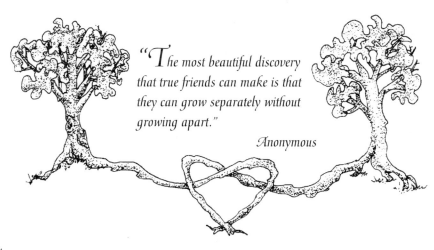

"The most beautiful discovery that true friends can make is that they can grow separately without growing apart."

Anonymous

Deluxe Oatmeal Cookies

$1/3$ cup ($5^1/3$ tablespoons) butter, softened
1 egg
$1/2$ teaspoon vanilla

1. Preheat oven to 350°. Empty contents of jar into large mixing bowl.
2. Add butter or margarine, egg and vanilla.
3. Beat on low speed until dough is thoroughly blended.
4. Roll heaping teaspoonfuls of dough into balls and place 3 inches apart on ungreased cookie sheet.
5. Bake for 12 to 14 minutes or until edges are lightly browned. Remove from oven and let cookies cool on cookie sheet for 1 minute before transferring to cooling rack. (Makes 3 to $3^1/2$ dozen.)

www.cookbookresources.com

Deluxe Oatmeal Cookies

$1/3$ cup ($5^1/3$ tablespoons) butter, softened
1 egg
$1/2$ teaspoon vanilla

1. Preheat oven to 350°. Empty contents of jar into large mixing bowl.
2. Add butter or margarine, egg and vanilla.
3. Beat on low speed until dough is thoroughly blended.
4. Roll heaping teaspoonfuls of dough into balls and place 3 inches apart on ungreased cookie sheet.
5. Bake for 12 to 14 minutes or until edges are lightly browned. Remove from oven and let cookies cool on cookie sheet for 1 minute before transferring to cooling rack. (Makes 3 to $3^1/2$ dozen.)

www.cookbookresources.com

Deluxe Oatmeal Cookies

$1/3$ cup ($5^1/3$ tablespoons) butter, softened
1 egg
$1/2$ teaspoon vanilla

1. Preheat oven to 350°. Empty contents of jar into large mixing bowl.
2. Add butter or margarine, egg and vanilla.
3. Beat on low speed until dough is thoroughly blended.
4. Roll heaping teaspoonfuls of dough into balls and place 3 inches apart on ungreased cookie sheet.
5. Bake for 12 to 14 minutes or until edges are lightly browned. Remove from oven and let cookies cool on cookie sheet for 1 minute before transferring to cooling rack. (Makes 3 to $3^1/2$ dozen.)

www.cookbookresources.com

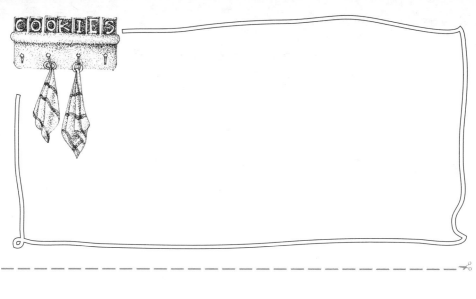

You're a Doll

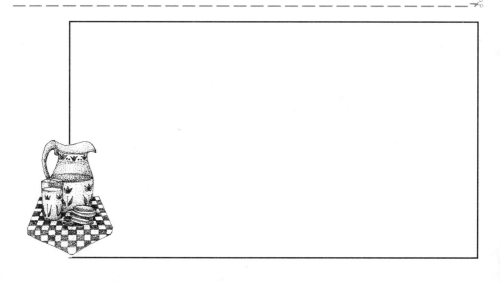

Deluxe Oatmeal Cookies

$^1/_3$ cup ($5^1/_3$ tablespoons) butter, softened
1 egg
$^1/_2$ teaspoon vanilla

1. Preheat oven to 350°. Empty contents of jar into large mixing bowl.
2. Add butter or margarine, egg and vanilla.
3. Beat on low speed until dough is thoroughly blended.
4. Roll heaping teaspoonfuls of dough into balls and place 3 inches apart on ungreased cookie sheet.
5. Bake for 12 to 14 minutes or until edges are lightly browned. Remove from oven and let cookies cool on cookie sheet for 1 minute before transferring to cooling rack. (Makes 3 to $3^1/_2$ dozen.)

www.cookbookresources.com

Deluxe Oatmeal Cookies

$^1/_3$ cup ($5^1/_3$ tablespoons) butter, softened
1 egg
$^1/_2$ teaspoon vanilla

1. Preheat oven to 350°. Empty contents of jar into large mixing bowl.
2. Add butter or margarine, egg and vanilla.
3. Beat on low speed until dough is thoroughly blended.
4. Roll heaping teaspoonfuls of dough into balls and place 3 inches apart on ungreased cookie sheet.
5. Bake for 12 to 14 minutes or until edges are lightly browned. Remove from oven and let cookies cool on cookie sheet for 1 minute before transferring to cooling rack. (Makes 3 to $3^1/_2$ dozen.)

www.cookbookresources.com

Deluxe Oatmeal Cookies

$^1/_3$ cup ($5^1/_3$ tablespoons) butter, softened
1 egg
$^1/_2$ teaspoon vanilla

1. Preheat oven to 350°. Empty contents of jar into large mixing bowl.
2. Add butter or margarine, egg and vanilla.
3. Beat on low speed until dough is thoroughly blended.
4. Roll heaping teaspoonfuls of dough into balls and place 3 inches apart on ungreased cookie sheet.
5. Bake for 12 to 14 minutes or until edges are lightly browned. Remove from oven and let cookies cool on cookie sheet for 1 minute before transferring to cooling rack. (Makes 3 to $3^1/_2$ dozen.)

www.cookbookresources.com

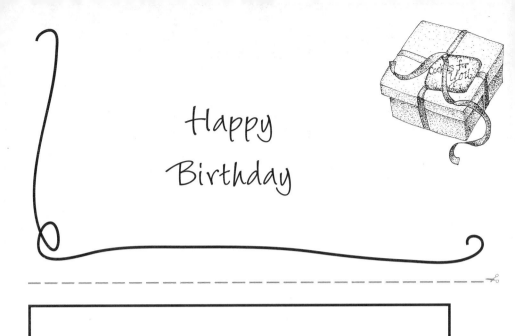

Happy
Birthday

Happy Holidays

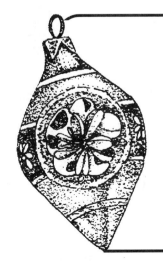

Merry Christmas

Molasses Cookies

Molasses Cookies

Robust molasses and spice flavor in a dark-colored cookie with a crunchy exterior make for a special taste treat.

Ingredients for jar:

1 cup packed dark brown sugar
3 cups flour
$1^1/_2$ teaspoons baking soda
1 tablespoon dried, grated orange peel*
1 teaspoon cinnamon
$^1/_2$ teaspoon ginger
$^1/_8$ teaspoon ground cloves
$^1/_4$ teaspoon allspice
$^1/_3$ cup chopped dates

Instructions for jar:

1. Place brown sugar in 1-quart jar and pack down firmly and evenly.
2. In medium bowl, combine flour with baking soda, orange peel, cinnamon, ginger, cloves and allspice. Stir well to mix.
3. Spoon flour mixture over brown sugar, pressing down with each addition.
4. Place dates over flour mixture and press down to fit all in jar. Place lid on jar to close.

*Dried, grated orange peel can be found in the spice section of your grocery store.

Molasses Cookies

Instructions for baking:

1 egg
1 cup (2 sticks) butter, softened
$^1/_2$ cup molasses
1 teaspoon vanilla

1. Preheat oven to 375°. Empty contents of jar into large mixing bowl.

2. Add egg, butter or margarine, molasses and vanilla. Beat on low speed or by hand until dough is thoroughly blended.

3. Drop by rounded teaspoonfuls onto ungreased cookie sheet. Bake for 7 to 9 minutes or until set. (Makes about 4 dozen.)

> "*How* lucky I am to have known someone who was so hard to say goodbye to."
>
> *Anonymous*

Molasses Cookies

1 egg
1 cup (2 sticks) butter, softened
1/2 cup molasses
1 teaspoon vanilla

1. Preheat oven to 375°. Empty contents of jar into large mixing bowl.
2. Add egg, butter or margarine, molasses and vanilla. Beat on low speed or by hand until dough is thoroughly blended.
3. Drop by rounded teaspoonfuls onto ungreased cookie sheet. Bake for 7 to 9 minutes or until set. (Makes about 4 dozen.)

www.cookbookresources.com

Molasses Cookies

1 egg
1 cup (2 sticks) butter, softened
1/2 cup molasses
1 teaspoon vanilla

1. Preheat oven to 375°. Empty contents of jar into large mixing bowl.
2. Add egg, butter or margarine, molasses and vanilla. Beat on low speed or by hand until dough is thoroughly blended.
3. Drop by rounded teaspoonfuls onto ungreased cookie sheet. Bake for 7 to 9 minutes or until set. (Makes about 4 dozen.)

www.cookbookresources.com

Molasses Cookies

1 egg
1 cup (2 sticks) butter, softened
1/2 cup molasses
1 teaspoon vanilla

1. Preheat oven to 375°. Empty contents of jar into large mixing bowl.
2. Add egg, butter or margarine, molasses and vanilla. Beat on low speed or by hand until dough is thoroughly blended.
3. Drop by rounded teaspoonfuls onto ungreased cookie sheet. Bake for 7 to 9 minutes or until set. (Makes about 4 dozen.)

www.cookbookresources.com

Thinking of You

Molasses Cookies

1 egg
1 cup (2 sticks) butter, softened
$^1/_2$ cup molasses
1 teaspoon vanilla

1. Preheat oven to 375°. Empty contents of jar into large mixing bowl.
2. Add egg, butter or margarine, molasses and vanilla. Beat on low speed or by hand until dough is thoroughly blended.
3. Drop by rounded teaspoonfuls onto ungreased cookie sheet. Bake for 7 to 9 minutes or until set. (Makes about 4 dozen.)

Molasses Cookies

1 egg
1 cup (2 sticks) butter, softened
$^1/_2$ cup molasses
1 teaspoon vanilla

1. Preheat oven to 375°. Empty contents of jar into large mixing bowl.
2. Add egg, butter or margarine, molasses and vanilla. Beat on low speed or by hand until dough is thoroughly blended.
3. Drop by rounded teaspoonfuls onto ungreased cookie sheet. Bake for 7 to 9 minutes or until set. (Makes about 4 dozen.)

www.cookbookresources.com

Molasses Cookies

1 egg
1 cup (2 sticks) butter, softened
$^1/_2$ cup molasses
1 teaspoon vanilla

1. Preheat oven to 375°. Empty contents of jar into large mixing bowl.
2. Add egg, butter or margarine, molasses and vanilla. Beat on low speed or by hand until dough is thoroughly blended.
3. Drop by rounded teaspoonfuls onto ungreased cookie sheet. Bake for 7 to 9 minutes or until set. (Makes about 4 dozen.)

www.cookbookresources.com

Happy Birthday

Happy Holidays

Merry Christmas

Butter Pecan Delights

Butter Pecan Delights

Everyone loves these beautiful round, lightly-colored cookies with the texture of shortbread, but sweeter and flavored with almond toffee and pecans. A wonderful combination!

Ingredients for jar:
1 cup sugar
2 cups flour
1 teaspoon baking powder
1 cup finely chopped or ground pecans
$1/2$ cup toffee chips for baking or crushed Heath candy bars

Instructions for jar:
1. Place sugar in 1-quart jar and smooth over.
2. Spoon flour and baking powder over sugar.
3. Place pecans on top of flour and press down evenly.
4. Sprinkle toffee chips over pecans. Place lid on jar and close.

Butter Pecan Delights
Instructions for baking:

1 cup (2 sticks) butter, softened
2 egg yolks

1. Preheat oven to 325°. Empty contents of jar into large mixing bowl.

2. Add butter or margarine and egg yolks.

3. Beat on low speed or by hand until dough is thoroughly blended.

4. Shape teaspoonfuls of dough into balls and place 2 inches apart on lightly greased cookie sheet.

5. Bake for 15 to 17 minutes or until very lightly brown. Remove from oven and let cool on cookie sheet for 1 minute, then transfer to cooling rack. (Makes $3^{1}/_{2}$ to 4 dozen.)

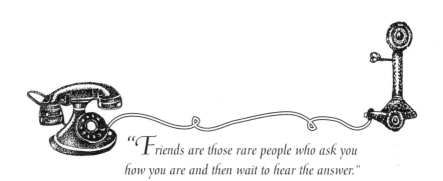

"Friends are those rare people who ask you how you are and then wait to hear the answer."

Anonymous

Butter Pecan Delights

1 cup (2 sticks) butter, softened
2 egg yolks

1. Preheat oven to 325°. Empty contents of jar into large mixing bowl.
2. Add butter or margarine and egg yolks.
3. Beat on low speed or by hand until dough is thoroughly blended.
4. Shape teaspoonfuls of dough into balls and place 2 inches apart on lightly greased cookie sheet.
5. Bake for 15 to 17 minutes or until very lightly brown. Remove from oven and let cool on cookie sheet for 1 minute, then transfer to cooling rack. (Makes $3^1/_2$ to 4 dozen.)

Butter Pecan Delights

1 cup (2 sticks) butter, softened
2 egg yolks

1. Preheat oven to 325°. Empty contents of jar into large mixing bowl.
2. Add butter or margarine and egg yolks.
3. Beat on low speed or by hand until dough is thoroughly blended.
4. Shape teaspoonfuls of dough into balls and place 2 inches apart on lightly greased cookie sheet.
5. Bake for 15 to 17 minutes or until very lightly brown. Remove from oven and let cool on cookie sheet for 1 minute, then transfer to cooling rack. (Makes $3^1/_2$ to 4 dozen.)

Butter Pecan Delights

1 cup (2 sticks) butter, softened
2 egg yolks

1. Preheat oven to 325°. Empty contents of jar into large mixing bowl.
2. Add butter or margarine and egg yolks.
3. Beat on low speed or by hand until dough is thoroughly blended.
4. Shape teaspoonfuls of dough into balls and place 2 inches apart on lightly greased cookie sheet.
5. Bake for 15 to 17 minutes or until very lightly brown. Remove from oven and let cool on cookie sheet for 1 minute, then transfer to cooling rack. (Makes $3^1/_2$ to 4 dozen.)

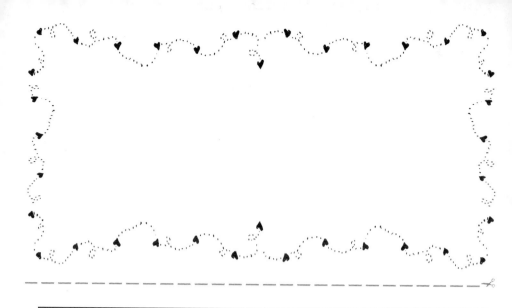

You're a Pal

Butter Pecan Delights

1 cup (2 sticks) butter, softened
2 egg yolks

1. Preheat oven to 325°. Empty contents of jar into large mixing bowl.
2. Add butter or margarine and egg yolks.
3. Beat on low speed or by hand until dough is thoroughly blended.
4. Shape teaspoonfuls of dough into balls and place 2 inches apart on lightly greased cookie sheet.
5. Bake for 15 to 17 minutes or until very lightly brown. Remove from oven and let cool on cookie sheet for 1 minute, then transfer to cooling rack. (Makes $3^1/_2$ to 4 dozen.)

www.cookbookresources.com

Butter Pecan Delights

1 cup (2 sticks) butter, softened
2 egg yolks

1. Preheat oven to 325°. Empty contents of jar into large mixing bowl.
2. Add butter or margarine and egg yolks.
3. Beat on low speed or by hand until dough is thoroughly blended.
4. Shape teaspoonfuls of dough into balls and place 2 inches apart on lightly greased cookie sheet.
5. Bake for 15 to 17 minutes or until very lightly brown. Remove from oven and let cool on cookie sheet for 1 minute, then transfer to cooling rack. (Makes $3^1/_2$ to 4 dozen.)

www.cookbookresources.com

Butter Pecan Delights

1 cup (2 sticks) butter, softened
2 egg yolks

1. Preheat oven to 325°. Empty contents of jar into large mixing bowl.
2. Add butter or margarine and egg yolks.
3. Beat on low speed or by hand until dough is thoroughly blended.
4. Shape teaspoonfuls of dough into balls and place 2 inches apart on lightly greased cookie sheet.
5. Bake for 15 to 17 minutes or until very lightly brown. Remove from oven and let cool on cookie sheet for 1 minute, then transfer to cooling rack. (Makes $3^1/_2$ to 4 dozen.)

www.cookbookresources.com

Happy Birthday

Happy Holidays

Merry Christmas

Chocolate Snickerdoodles

Chocolate Snickerdoodles

This is a spin on an old favorite: chocolate-flavored cookies coated with cinnamon and sugar.

Ingredients for jar:

$1\,^1/_3$ cups sugar

$^1/_4$ cup cocoa powder

$1\,^3/_4$ cups flour

$^1/_2$ teaspoon baking powder

$^3/_4$ cup finely chopped or ground pecans

Instructions for jar:

1. Place sugar in 1-quart jar and smooth over.
2. Gently spoon cocoa powder evenly over sugar.
3. Spoon flour and baking powder over cocoa, pressing down lightly.
4. Add pecans to jar on top of flour and press down firmly. Place lid on jar to close.

Chocolate Snickerdoodles
Instructions for baking:

1 egg
³/₄ cup (1¹/₂ sticks) butter, softened
2 tablespoons milk
1 teaspoon vanilla
3 tablespoons sugar
1¹/₂ teaspoons cinnamon

1. Preheat oven to 375°. Empty contents of jar into large mixing bowl.

2. Add egg, butter or margarine, milk and vanilla.

3. Beat on low speed or by hand until dough is thoroughly blended. Cover dough and refrigerate for 1 hour.

4. In small bowl, combine 3 tablespoons sugar and 1¹/₂ teaspoons cinnamon. Stir to completely mix.

5. Take pieces of dough and roll into 1-inch balls. Roll balls in the sugar-cinnamon mixture and place 2 inches apart on ungreased cookie sheet.

6. Bake for 10 to 11 minutes or until lightly browned around edges. Remove from oven and let cookies cool on cookie sheet for 1 minute, then transfer to cooling rack. (Makes about 4 dozen.)

"Friends are the angels who lift us to our feet when our wings have trouble remembering how to fly."

Anonymous

Chocolate Snickerdoodles

1 egg
3/4 cup (1 1/2 sticks) butter, softened
2 tablespoons milk

1 teaspoon vanilla
3 tablespoons sugar
1 1/2 teaspoons cinnamon

1. Preheat oven to 375°. Empty contents of jar into large mixing bowl.
2. Add egg, butter or margarine, milk and vanilla.
3. Beat on low speed or by hand until dough is thoroughly blended. Cover dough and refrigerate for 1 hour.
4. In small bowl, combine 3 tablespoons sugar and 1 1/2 teaspoons cinnamon. Stir to completely mix.
5. Take pieces of dough and roll into 1-inch balls. Roll balls in the sugar-cinnamon mixture and place 2 inches apart on ungreased cookie sheet.
6. Bake for 10 to 11 minutes or until lightly browned around edges. Remove from oven and let cookies cool on cookie sheet for 1 minute, then transfer to cooling rack. (Makes about 4 dozen.)

www.cookbookresources.com

Chocolate Snickerdoodles

1 egg
3/4 cup (1 1/2 sticks) butter, softened
2 tablespoons milk

1 teaspoon vanilla
3 tablespoons sugar
1 1/2 teaspoons cinnamon

1. Preheat oven to 375°. Empty contents of jar into large mixing bowl.
2. Add egg, butter or margarine, milk and vanilla.
3. Beat on low speed or by hand until dough is thoroughly blended. Cover dough and refrigerate for 1 hour.
4. In small bowl, combine 3 tablespoons sugar and 1 1/2 teaspoons cinnamon. Stir to completely mix.
5. Take pieces of dough and roll into 1-inch balls. Roll balls in the sugar-cinnamon mixture and place 2 inches apart on ungreased cookie sheet.
6. Bake for 10 to 11 minutes or until lightly browned around edges. Remove from oven and let cookies cool on cookie sheet for 1 minute, then transfer to cooling rack. (Makes about 4 dozen.)

www.cookbookresources.com

Chocolate Snickerdoodles

1 egg
3/4 cup (1 1/2 sticks) butter, softened
2 tablespoons milk

1 teaspoon vanilla
3 tablespoons sugar
1 1/2 teaspoons cinnamon

1. Preheat oven to 375°. Empty contents of jar into large mixing bowl.
2. Add egg, butter or margarine, milk and vanilla.
3. Beat on low speed or by hand until dough is thoroughly blended. Cover dough and refrigerate for 1 hour.
4. In small bowl, combine 3 tablespoons sugar and 1 1/2 teaspoons cinnamon. Stir to completely mix.
5. Take pieces of dough and roll into 1-inch balls. Roll balls in the sugar-cinnamon mixture and place 2 inches apart on ungreased cookie sheet.
6. Bake for 10 to 11 minutes or until lightly browned around edges. Remove from oven and let cookies cool on cookie sheet for 1 minute, then transfer to cooling rack. (Makes about 4 dozen.)

www.cookbookresources.com

Best Wishes

Chocolate Snickerdoodles

1 egg	1 teaspoon vanilla
$^3/_4$ cup ($1^1/_2$ sticks) butter, softened	3 tablespoons sugar
2 tablespoons milk	$1^1/_2$ teaspoons cinnamon

1. Preheat oven to 375°. Empty contents of jar into large mixing bowl.
2. Add egg, butter or margarine, milk and vanilla.
3. Beat on low speed or by hand until dough is thoroughly blended. Cover dough and refrigerate for 1 hour.
4. In small bowl, combine 3 tablespoons sugar and $1^1/_2$ teaspoons cinnamon. Stir to completely mix.
5. Take pieces of dough and roll into 1-inch balls. Roll balls in the sugar-cinnamon mixture and place 2 inches apart on ungreased cookie sheet.
6. Bake for 10 to 11 minutes or until lightly browned around edges. Remove from oven and let cookies cool on cookie sheet for 1 minute, then transfer to cooling rack. (Makes about 4 dozen.)

www.cookbookresources.com

Chocolate Snickerdoodles

1 egg	1 teaspoon vanilla
$^3/_4$ cup ($1^1/_2$ sticks) butter, softened	3 tablespoons sugar
2 tablespoons milk	$1^1/_2$ teaspoons cinnamon

1. Preheat oven to 375°. Empty contents of jar into large mixing bowl.
2. Add egg, butter or margarine, milk and vanilla.
3. Beat on low speed or by hand until dough is thoroughly blended. Cover dough and refrigerate for 1 hour.
4. In small bowl, combine 3 tablespoons sugar and $1^1/_2$ teaspoons cinnamon. Stir to completely mix.
5. Take pieces of dough and roll into 1-inch balls. Roll balls in the sugar-cinnamon mixture and place 2 inches apart on ungreased cookie sheet.
6. Bake for 10 to 11 minutes or until lightly browned around edges. Remove from oven and let cookies cool on cookie sheet for 1 minute, then transfer to cooling rack. (Makes about 4 dozen.)

www.cookbookresources.com

Chocolate Snickerdoodles

1 egg	1 teaspoon vanilla
$^3/_4$ cup ($1^1/_2$ sticks) butter, softened	3 tablespoons sugar
2 tablespoons milk	$1^1/_2$ teaspoons cinnamon

1. Preheat oven to 375°. Empty contents of jar into large mixing bowl.
2. Add egg, butter or margarine, milk and vanilla.
3. Beat on low speed or by hand until dough is thoroughly blended. Cover dough and refrigerate for 1 hour.
4. In small bowl, combine 3 tablespoons sugar and $1^1/_2$ teaspoons cinnamon. Stir to completely mix.
5. Take pieces of dough and roll into 1-inch balls. Roll balls in the sugar-cinnamon mixture and place 2 inches apart on ungreased cookie sheet.
6. Bake for 10 to 11 minutes or until lightly browned around edges. Remove from oven and let cookies cool on cookie sheet for 1 minute, then transfer to cooling rack. (Makes about 4 dozen.)

www.cookbookresources.com

Happy Birthday

Happy Holidays

Merry Christmas

Cookie Jar Gift Reference

Date	Name of Recipient	Name of Cookie Given

Cookie Jar Gift Reference

Date	Name of Recipient	Name of Cookie Given

Cookbooks Published By Cookbook Resources

Easy Cooking With 5 Ingredients
The Ultimate Cooking With 4 Ingredients
The Best of Cooking With 3 Ingredients
Easy Gourmet Cooking With 5 Ingredients
Healthy Cooking With 4 Ingredients
Easy Slow-Cooker Cooking With 4 Ingredients
Easy Dessert Cooking With 5 Ingredients
Quick Fixes With Mixes
Casseroles To The Rescue
Kitchen Keepsakes/More Kitchen Keepsakes
Mother's Recipes
Recipe Keepsakes
Cookie Dough Secrets
Gifts For The Cookie Jar
Cookbook 25 Years
Pass The Plate
Texas Longhorn Cookbook
Mealtimes and Memories
Holiday Treats
Homecoming
Cookin' With Will Rogers
Best of Lone Star Legacy Cookbook
Little Taste of Texas
Little Taste of Texas II
Southwest Sizzler
Southwest Ole
Classroom Treats
Leaving Home

cookbook
resources LLC
www.cookbookresources.com

To Order Cookie Jar Magic:

Please send_____ copies @ $19.95 (U.S.) each $_____

Plus postage/handling @ $6.00 each $_____

Texas residents add sales tax @ $1.48 each $_____

Check or Credit Card (Canada-credit card only) **Total** $_____

Charge to my ☐ **VISA** or ☐ **MasterCard**

Account #_____

Expiration Date_____

Signature_____

Mail or Call:
Cookbook Resour ces
541 Doubletr ee Drive
Highland V illage, TX 75077
Toll-fr ee: 866/229-2665
972/317-0245
www.cookbookr esources.com

Name_____

Address_____

City_____State_____Zip_____

Phone (day)_____ (night)_____

- -

To Order Cookie Jar Magic:

Please send_____ copies @ $19.95 (U.S.) each $_____

Plus postage/handling @ $6.00 each $_____

Texas residents add sales tax @ $1.48 each $_____

Check or Credit Card (Canada-credit card only) **Total** $_____

Charge to my ☐ **VISA** or ☐ **MasterCard**

Account #_____

Expiration Date_____

Signature_____

Mail or Call:
Cookbook Resour ces
541 Doubletr ee Drive
Highland V illage, TX 75077
Toll-fr ee: 866/229-2665
972/317-0245
www.cookbookr esources.com

Name_____

Address_____

City_____State_____Zip_____

Phone (day)_____ (night)_____